Enjoy your journey!

ACCLAIM FOR *BELIEVABLE*

"Does God truly *desire* to save all? Is God *able* to reconcile all to himself? Do the Scriptures *foresee* ultimate redemption? J. D. Atkinson joins the rising chorus of voices whose *Yes!* is a glorious harmony of praise to the One who said, 'If I am lifted up, I SHALL draw ALL people to myself.' The author's radical proposal is that Jesus was not mistaken, human defiance and forthcoming judgments notwithstanding. What makes John David's contribution to the orchestra special is that his theo-logic and his faithfulness to Scripture are so incredibly accessible that it's impossible to miss his point... or Christ's good news message!"

— BRADLEY JERSAK, Dean of Theology & Culture,
St. Stephen's University (New Brunswick),
Author of *Her Gates Will Never Be Shut*

"BELIEVABLE by J. D. Atkinson is a must-read for anyone wanting to better understand what lies ahead after this life has ended. It's a short and easy read, yet it contains so many key thoughts presented in a concise, logical, and compelling manner. The author approaches the subject from a philosophical perspective, from a review of the Scriptures, from a look at church history, and—most importantly—from the experiences of life and common sense. The conclusion is one that is not commonly heard in the churches of our day, which present a gospel that contains more of the 'traditions of man' than the truth God has presented in the Holy Scriptures. So those sitting in a church pew week after week are never really exposed to a most powerful truth and the core of God's message to mankind: that He is in the process of saving and reconciling *all*, not just some. For those never exposed to this truth, this book will challenge you with many thought-provoking questions, and with conclusions that are backed up by significant and compelling evidence. So pick up this book, carve out some time, and dive in. You will not be disappointed—and you may be surprised at the plans of God that are presently underway."

— BOB EVELY, Former United Methodist Church Pastor,
Author of *At The End of the Ages*

"BELIEVABLE is a fantastic achievement: It's a year-long seminary Apologetics course in an easy-to-follow book of just over 200 pages! Unlike almost every apologetics book written about Christian Universalism, BELIEVABLE not only shows that 'Through Christ, God reconciles

all to Himself,' but also that this truly Good News is inseparable from
the rest of the Christian message. J.D. Atkinson has made a very
significant contribution to showing that the reconciliation of all to God
is the core of the Gospel."

— DR. LANCE W. HAVERKAMP, Executive Minister,
Christian Universalist Association

"I find J.D. Atkinson's book BELIEVABLE, to be, above all, interesting
and thoughtful. It is easy to read, yet substantial. As an introductory
work centered upon the cause of Christ, it affords the careful reader
considerable insight into the things of God. One of the most noteworthy,
and indeed, 'worthy of all welcome' (cf 1 Tim.4:9) things among the
things of God, may be found in the testimony of the apostle Paul where
he declares, 'God ... wills that all humanity be saved and come into
a realization of the truth' (1 Tim.2:3b,4). This is to say that *God has
formed the decision to save all mankind;* and, He is continuing on in
this selfsame resolve unto the realization of this very goal. It needs to
be recognized that any issues concerning the nature of human choice
simply have no bearing on the theme of the saving work of Christ. This
is because, considered at its deepest level, salvation is without fail a
matter of *gratuitous grace,* not of qualification or reward. Boasting in
man, then, is debarred; to God alone be the glory."

— JAMES CORAM, President,
Concordant Publishing Concern

"BELIEVABLE is about human life: its source, purpose and destiny. The
author's claims are credible because of the authority of his witnesses:
science, reason and the Bible. I have read many books defending the
truth of Jesus as our 'successful' savior, but none has pieced together
so many thoughts and facts from such a wide spectrum of topical
evidence: from creation to the historical Jesus (no one can walk away
saying, 'Jesus was just a myth'); his life on earth; his death and what
it meant; to his resurrection and glory in the age to come! J.D. shows
how all God's judgments work for good, harmonizing perfectly with his
mercy on all. He includes all the relevant issues concisely, yet makes
it very enjoyable to read for everyone—teenager and scholar alike. Just
amazing!"

— GERRY BEAUCHEMIN,
Author of *Hope Beyond Hell*

BELIEVABLE

DISCOVER THE GOD THAT SAVES ALL

J. D. Atkinson

Published by Decycle
Navasota, Texas, USA
www.decycle.com

Library of Congress Control Number: 2023923698

ISBN 978-1-7366571-0-2   Hardcover
ISBN 978-1-7366571-1-9   Paperback
ISBN 978-1-7366571-2-6   eBook
ISBN 978-1-7366571-3-3   Audiobook

10   9   8   7   6   5   4   3   2   1

For my Dad, who always loves and never gives up

CONTENTS

INTRODUCTION

I SPENT decades in the dark. A religious system had me convinced that God looked upon me with favor, while everyone else was not so fortunate. Almost all mainstream religions are based on this pretense. Without an exclusive offer of paradise, few would convert.

Maybe it's the essence of being human to assume we've got it figured out. I sure felt that way. But if we're lucky, someone will come along to shake things up and challenge our views.

For me, that someone was my father.

Years ago, he stumbled upon older writings that diverged from what we were being taught by today's religious leaders. They spoke of a God who loved his creatures equally—enough to save every last one. Together we set out to debunk that claim. In the end, however, we had no choice but to embrace it. The message was so logical—and so *evident*—that we were shocked we'd never heard it before.

There is nothing new under the sun, and this information is no exception. It has been hiding in plain sight for centuries, obscured by the darkness of today's popular dualistic theology.

My hope is that you'll find this book thought provoking. But my prayer is that, like me, you'll discover a truth you didn't even realize was missing: that God really is "the Savior of all people," just as he claims.

J. D. ATKINSON

CHAPTER 1

LIFE

To live is the rarest thing in the world.
Most people exist, that is all.

— OSCAR WILDE

YOU ARE DYING. Like a battery, your life began fully charged. But it started draining the moment you took your first breath. The difference between human beings and batteries is that we can't be recharged. When we run out, it's game over.

Time seems to accelerate with each passing decade. The years slip by like sand through our fingers. If we're lucky, we grow old—but one day our time will be up. Every single life is counting down to its scheduled expiration date.

Some will try to leave a legacy. But our great-grandchildren probably won't care what kind of cars we drove, how beautiful our homes were, or how well-respected we were in our professions. In time, those achievements become meaningless.

Even if mankind could live forever, this planet cannot. Someday the earth's natural resources will be exhausted. If we do not self-destruct through war, our sun will eventually grow hotter and larger until Earth is either uninhabitable or consumed by fire. Even moving to a neighboring galaxy would not prevent the ever-expanding universe from ultimately entering a state of heat death due to entropy.[1]

There is no escape. No matter where we go or what we do, death lies ahead.

CHOICES, CHOICES

Have you ever heard someone ask, "Why do bad things happen to good people?" Maybe you've wondered that yourself. Both good and bad things happen to everyone: wealth and poverty, joy and despair, health and sickness—these can touch any of us, regardless of how we behave or the choices we make.

Consider the multitude of children diagnosed with terminal illnesses each year. The combination of DNA from each parent may result in unfavorable genetic mutations. Chemicals, pesticides, and medications a mother comes into contact with during pregnancy can adversely affect her baby's development. Polluted food and water supplies also contribute to disease. These innocent children didn't do anything to deserve sickness.

However, many of the difficulties we face are the direct consequences of our own poor choices, factors we have the power to control. Our decisions have an enormous impact on our lives, the lives of those around us, and our children—often for several generations. Realizing this, we usually try to make good choices.

When we face a significant decision, we sometimes sense that we are part of something much larger. We catch brief glimpses of a bigger picture, a greater goal, a common good. We may perceive one option as good and the other bad, but we are always free to choose our own path.

The freedom to make choices comes with a catch: it requires owning the results. In the end, we may either appreciate or regret our decisions and the consequences. But if someone else were to intervene and mitigate the effect of our choice—say, by limiting the joy or pain it brings—our choice would be meaningless. Without reaping the consequences, there is no freedom to choose. This is why our choices must freely result in either smiles or tears, joy or sorrow.

ONE'S RIGHT IS ANOTHER'S WRONG

If a person believes that life is just an accident and there is no creator, a logical goal would be unrestrained self-indulgence.

In the jungle, there is no code of ethics. Animals know neither mercy nor the golden rule. Someone who believes life is a random accident may as well behave like an animal. He is free to act like a psychopath, engaging in every selfish pleasure he can conjure. If he maximizes his enjoyment at the cost of others by deceiving, murdering, and stealing, he should be proud that he did his best and played the game well. He may reason that his opponents shouldn't have let their guard down, or his intelligence or wealth make him superior. For him, preying on the weak is not shameful; exploitation of opportunity is the key to enjoying this brief life.

Thinly veiled variations of this psychotic mind-set are a recurrent theme in modern magazines, self-help books, and business publications focused solely on achieving one's own "success" or "happiness," whatever that may be, and no matter what it costs others. But the happy ending never materializes.

Between 1978 and 1991, a Wisconsin man by the name of Jeffrey Dahmer raped, murdered, and dismembered seventeen young male victims, some of whom he ate. When asked what contributed to his behavior he cited a lack of belief in God, which he admitted "cheapens life." He went on to say that "If a person doesn't think that there is a God to be accountable to, then what's the point of trying to modify your behavior to keep it within acceptable ranges? That's how I thought, anyway."[2]

I am not suggesting that humans need to believe in a supreme being to keep themselves from assaulting or eating each other.

But if there is no God, those who exercise moral restraint are only doing so for fear of an imaginary deity. If no supreme being exists, each individual is his own final authority. And if a man answers only to himself, why can't he live as he pleases? What makes Mr. Dahmer's desires any less valid than another person's desire to live in peace?

Mr. Dahmer's peers valued the lives of his victims much more than he did: he was sentenced to sixteen life terms in prison.[3]

Does our entire existence come down to survival of the fittest? Is our only function to kill or be killed? To pillage and plunder for our own amusement, before someone else gets us first? Are we all just animals that have come into being by chance?

Some have suggested that mankind is simply the product of random circumstances. But if that is the case, what is the basis for our collective moral code that chose to avenge Dahmer's victims? Why do we expect others to behave a certain way?

Why value honesty and equity? Why, since the dawn of time, has humanity failed to keep the very rules they *choose* to set? Who can really define what is right or wrong?

If our existence is the result of accidental or random forces, there is no logical reason for doing good deeds at the expense of our own self-gratification. Man-made concepts of right and wrong have no objective basis if there is no final authority other than ourselves. If each person is the ultimate judge of their own actions, then morality is a fluid, subjective fabrication of the mind. All that matters is what each person *feels* is right.

Jeffrey Dahmer believed that "we all just came from the slime and when we died, you know, that was it—there was nothing." Deep down, though, he questioned these things: as he lay face-down during his arrest, he said, "For what I did I should be dead."[4]

He had shown absolute disregard for the lives of his victims, yet even the brutal Mr. Dahmer had trouble believing that he alone was the final authority.

WHAT'S THE POINT?

Why are we here? What is the purpose of life?

There are endless theories to explain how we got here. It isn't possible to delve into each one, let alone expose their fallacies. Rather than analyzing a predefined worldview, the following chapters will start from nothing. We will rely on common sense to find the most reasonable explanations for observable facts. And in the interest of brevity, centuries of heated debate over various topics are distilled down to single chapters.

Everyone is in search of the truth. But how will we know when we've finally found it?

CHAPTER 2

LOGIC

*When dealing with people, remember you are not dealing
with creatures of logic, but with creatures bristling with
prejudice and motivated by pride and vanity.*

— DALE CARNEGIE

H UMANS are certainly creatures of habit. We make up our
minds quickly, and then stand by our choices. We tend to
filter information in a manner that helps us prove to ourselves
what we've already decided is true. This is why people often react
defensively when their views are challenged.

Consider our preferences for something trivial, like a favorite
soft drink, vehicle, or sports team. Someone else may argue that
their choice is superior, and it may be—but our minds are already
made up. *Mine is better than yours.* Many of these preferences are
picked up in childhood. Some are adopted from mentors or those
we admire. But once established, we rarely engage in a genuine
reassessment based on the merits.

When it comes to small decisions like soft drinks, the cars we
like, or which team to cheer for, personal preferences don't make
much difference. We have our favorites, and we enjoy discussing

them. However, the human tendency to "decide and defend" can be dangerous when it comes to ideologies. For example, it is quite common to only consider evidence that agrees with our existing beliefs. This is called *confirmation bias*, and it is the reason some of us are unable to have an enlightening discussion with those who hold different views—particularly on the topics of politics and religion. Such closely guarded ideals may form the fabric of one's identity. Challenging these constructs may give rise to anxiety, which can manifest in the form of anger, defensiveness, or a haughty "agreement to disagree." What should have been intriguing dialogue based on mutual understanding is interpreted as a threat instead. If we've done our due diligence and are truly confident in our conclusions, why act defensively?

The truth is that some people have no desire to learn. They have chosen to reject observable facts that challenge their existing views. Are they afraid? Tired of thinking critically? Regardless, they have decided to squander the gift of intelligent reason.

People like that aren't searching for the truth. They've already constructed a personal reality. Maybe it's a comfortable position, or they feel pressure to think a certain way. Perhaps it gives them a feeling of superiority. Or maybe they've stood by it for so long that they aren't willing to reconsider. Whatever the case, they have no genuine desire to explore alternatives. And once defending a position takes priority over discovering the truth, learning can no longer take place. They are stuck.

All of us are susceptible to closed-mindedness, and dogma can infect anyone. Although an atheist may claim he has no religion to defend, he is really no different from the religious zealot he persecutes: he has no proof of his position, yet argues as if it were fact—and may even ridicule those who believe differently.

Some are reluctant to accept the possibility of a higher power. Maybe they think the afterlife is a myth created to encourage us to behave. Many have seen the damage wrought by world religions that bring more destruction than peace. It can be hard to believe that a loving God would allow so much evil to exist. But choosing to reject a possibility from the outset prevents fair judgment—so as you seek answers, I urge you to resist the temptation to defend old opinions. Always approach new information with an open mind. Weigh the evidence carefully. If you do, you are likely to discover answers that make more sense.

REASON IS A SKILL

Computers are a source of both amazement and annoyance. But as powerful and useful as they are, they still require very detailed instructions. You must tell them, step by step, exactly what to do. Otherwise, they will do something... else. Or nothing at all.

The process of writing instructions for a computer to execute is called *programming* or *coding*. If you've never attempted to program a computer, you haven't experienced true frustration! Coding an application is extremely tedious, and the program will crash if your instructions contain even the tiniest mistake.

This is because computers do *exactly* what you tell them to. They execute their instructions with perfect precision. Their work is not affected by how they feel each day, or whether they had breakfast. They don't give bad answers due to personal financial struggles, office politics, or marital conflict. Computers are never fazed by feelings.

Our capacity for critical thinking hinges on the ability to set aside feelings—at least temporarily—to consider new data and to objectively assimilate facts. If we allow our feelings to short circuit the decision-making process, we will likely arrive at flawed conclusions and wrong beliefs.

When a computer encounters a problem, it lets us know by interrupting our work with a scary error message. It refuses to continue until we address the problem. Humans, however, may spend years constructing a system of false beliefs. We often form opinions within a bubble, comfortably isolated from opposing views and information. Rarely will others directly challenge us or speak truth to our errors. Even when we sense we're wrong, we tend to defend our positions, too proud to admit failure. Unfortunately, in real life, we get no such warning when our reasoning is flawed. We won't see a pop-up message in the bathroom mirror to tell us we're on the wrong track.

Poor decisions are often based on emotions rather than facts. Those who allow feelings to govern their choices are typically unhappy, unreliable, or untrustworthy. They often act on urges and desires rather than making objective decisions. They make choices they would never advise someone else to make. They are doing exactly as they please... yet they are miserable.

Self-indulgence breeds chaos, destruction, and failure. On the other hand, self-discipline yields peace, balance, and success. This undeniable truth applies to parents, athletes, pop stars, students, CEOs, politicians—everyone. And everyone knows it, too: If an intensely trained fighter squared off with a procrastinating slob in the boxing ring, which would you place your bet on? Would you rather have your vehicle repaired by a corner-cutting crook, or an honest mechanic? Would you prefer your surgeon to be a pill-popping comic, or the straight-laced professional that graduated first in his class? We choose those who make good choices.

Our ability to recognize virtue in others is easy, but it's the application in our own lives that proves difficult. Emotions are very powerful. They can be used to justify whatever we wish to do, even if it is a poor decision and we know it.

That is why objective reasoning is so important. It is the sole basis for everyday problem-solving. Thinking logically helps us to avoid trouble. It mitigates the baggage we unwittingly bring to the table. It lets us properly evaluate all options, rather than choosing based on how we feel in the moment. And it is a skill we can practice and improve. The more we avoid making decisions based solely on feelings, the better off we are: good judgment leads to a happier, healthier, more productive life.

While good reasoning is certainly beneficial when making life choices, it is absolutely critical in deciding what to believe. That's because sound logic is the only way to arrive at the truth.

FEELINGS DON'T MAKE IT TRUE

Some religious groups have convinced their followers that God is like a genie in a bottle. If they just have enough faith—or maybe donate enough money—God will give them anything they ask for. Though it sounds appealing, this teaching violates observable reality. Most remain poor and sick; all will die.

Other leaders question the authenticity of those who fail to demonstrate certain spiritual gifts. Some claim that those who aren't submerged in water during baptism are destined for hell. Others promise exact returns on donations, such as sevenfold or tenfold. Some invoke the handling of snakes or drinking poison to prove God's power. Others have pretended to heal their followers on stage, only to be exposed in great detail.[1]

False teachings like these could be refuted easily, if it weren't for the strong emotions they evoke.

Adherents to flawed beliefs will point to a few passages in a holy book in defense of their positions, but the rest of the world remains unconvinced. It's far more likely that well-intentioned followers are simply in too deep to turn back now. Maybe there's a warm fuzzy feeling resulting from misplaced hope, or a strong emotional high that interferes with the ability to confront reality. Intense or euphoric spiritual feelings are likely to prevent a logical assessment of the underlying belief.

And the same thing can even happen with *bad* feelings, too. Desperation has led many to take drastic steps in an effort to fix relationships, eliminate debt, or ensure a happy afterlife. Many fear that if they dare question what they're being taught, their hopes will be dashed—and they'll be out of options. Whether good or bad, strong feelings leave little room for reason.

Something worth believing should withstand the test of logic. Yet some religious leaders seem to want their followers to check their brains in at the door, accept everything they're told, and ask no questions.

What would you think if a group of people wearing black sweat suits and sneakers tried to convince you to wash down poison pills with liquor, and slip a plastic bag over your head in order to board a UFO flown by aliens behind a comet? Insane, right? And yet, in 1997, a group called Heaven's Gate committed suicide together in this way.[2]

We cannot simply rely on what other people tell us. Blind faith isn't the way to find the truth. It can only be found through sound reasoning. If you really want to find the truth, test everything you hear. Does it make sense? Does it violate observable facts?

Don't let emotions hinder your ability to reason. Powerful as they may be, feelings don't make something true.

REALITY CHECK

A boy who doesn't fully understand gravity may think flight is only a set of homemade wings away, but his father knows better. One is excited about the prospect of flying; the other is grounded in reality. Both may wholeheartedly believe their conclusions, but only one is operating with the advantage of facts on his side.

Facts narrow the possibilities and inform our views. The more facts we learn, the closer our perceptions will be to reality. The goal, of course, is to bring these two into perfect alignment.

In the process of learning, we must be vigilant to guard against accepting misinformation as fact. If something we accept along the way is false, we will build more incorrect information on top of it. Even if the steps past that point are accurate, the conclusion will be flawed. For example, you can study math all you want, but if you start from the premise that 1+1=3, then many of your answers are going to be wrong. A bold willingness to question everything you have previously accepted as true will bring you much closer to reality as you search for the truth.

If you've stayed awake for more than twenty-four hours (or if you have children!), you have experienced fatigue. At some point we must sleep. Without rest we cannot function normally. Sleep deprivation has been linked to impaired cognitive function, depression, mania, illness, and even death.[3]

Imagine if someone tried to convince you that you don't need sleep. "Sleep is a myth," they might say. "People who think they need it are just gullible and weak-minded." This is, of course, nonsense: the body's requirement for sleep doesn't simply vanish for those who change their opinion. It is an easily observable fact.

Yet similar arguments have been used to assert that there is no God: "Belief in a higher power is a sign of frailty," some say. "People worship gods out of guilt, weakness, or ignorance." And, of course, "Good people don't need religion."

But these are merely opinions. If they would like to defend their conclusion, they should cite logical reasons. Our opinions have absolutely no bearing on whether a higher power exists.

While belief in God may bring peace to the believer, a good feeling doesn't prove it is correct. And the reverse is also true: a belief isn't false simply because it brings people comfort.

Some choose to embrace certain views, while others choose to reject them. In this regard, a religious zealot's fervent belief in God is no different from an atheist's desire to reject it; both have found peace. But we're not looking for peace, we're looking for the truth—and reality doesn't change based on our opinion.

ONE REALITY

Regardless of what you may choose to believe about how your life began, each person's family history is fixed. Your parents' identities, backgrounds, appearances, and DNA; your conception, birth, and upbringing—none of this changes as a result of your knowledge or ignorance. Whether you believe it or not, there will always be one true account of your past.

If someone wrote a biography of your life, but spelled your mother's name wrong, that part would be incorrect. And what if they led others to believe your parents were extraterrestrials? Would your history change as a result? Of course not.

Yet, when it comes to other topics, we hear similar claims:

"Perception is reality."

"We can all have different concepts of the truth."

"My reality may be different from yours."

These ideas may sound appealing at first, but they are absurd. There is only one reality. The immutable events of the past will never be altered by our present perceptions.

Just like our personal history, the history of the universe is fixed. There is only one factual account that explains how it—and we—came to be. Any other explanation is incorrect.

QUESTIONS HUMANS ASK

The same mysteries mankind has pondered throughout history continue to baffle us today. Countless theories attempt to answer the same age-old philosophical questions about our origin and purpose:

- How did we get here? Were we created?

- If so, does the creator care? Why allow suffering?

- Has the creator lost control?

We have no way to definitively answer some questions. However, if we apply sound reason to incontrovertible evidence, we can rule out many ideas and quickly narrow our focus to the most reasonable explanations.

CHAPTER 3

RELIGIONS

The easy confidence with which I know another man's religion is folly teaches me to suspect that my own is also.

— MARK TWAIN

I N JULY 2014, child-protection workers in the state of Georgia discovered a thirteen-year-old boy locked in an eight-by-six-foot room in his parents' basement. The room had only a bed and a bucket to relieve himself in—no light bulb, television, books, or toys. The window had been painted over. Though the boy appeared to be in good health, he had allegedly been in solitary confinement for more than a year.[1]

His parents, a devout religious couple who seemed to love all their children very much, had locked their oldest son in the basement for "disciplinary reasons." They were subsequently charged with child cruelty and false imprisonment. No doubt there are better ways to correct a child's behavior than that, no matter the offense. Yet, deplorable as it may be, such treatment is very mild compared to what some say God is going to do to many of us.

John Calvin (1509–1564) is one of most influential theologians of all time. He taught there is nothing people can do to change their final destiny because it has already been chosen for them: some will go to hell, and some will go to heaven—not because of anything they did, but simply because God had already chosen his favorites before any of us were even born. In his most notable and authoritative work, *Institutes of the Christian Religion*, Calvin explained his beliefs:

> [God] has determined in himself, what he would have to become of every individual of mankind. For they are not all created with a similar destiny; but eternal life is foreordained for some, and eternal damnation for others. Every man, therefore, being created for one or the other of these ends, we say, he is predestinated either to life or to death.[2]

According to this philosophy, getting into heaven is a random lottery. God, the winning team captain, "saves whom he will of his mere good pleasure," and man's choices and actions have no bearing on the outcome.[3]

God's selection of favorites, Calvin claims, "is founded on his gratuitous mercy, totally irrespective of human merit; but that to those whom he devotes to condemnation, the gate of life is closed by a just and irreprehensible, but incomprehensible, judgment."[4]

And just what is this judgment that awaits the vast majority of mankind? It is mentioned in many works, including *The Saints' Everlasting Rest*, penned in 1650 by Richard Baxter. This revered Christian classic describes it in graphic detail:

> Is it not a terrible thing to a wretched soul, when it shall lie roaring perpetually in the flames of hell, and the God of mercy himself shall laugh at them? When they shall cry out for mercy, yea, for one drop of water, and God shall mock them instead of relieving them? When none in heaven or earth can help them but God, and he shall rejoice over them in their calamity?[5]

This, we are told, is the behavior of a just and loving God, and to question his authority to do as he pleases is blasphemy. We are often reminded that God brought each person into this world, and he alone has the right to do with them as he pleases.

Of course, most Christian denominations will assert that man *does* have a choice with regard to the afterlife. But this is no less troubling. Is mankind equipped to make such a crucial decision? It is akin to requiring preschoolers to select their professions at age three, then holding them to their choice indefinitely. And compared to an omniscient deity, we are like children. We are told we must make the most pivotal choice of our existence—while operating at the most severe disadvantage imaginable—and that God will never give us a second chance.

God, we are told, is both loving and just. But that is neither.

Imagine a father standing at a busy intersection with his young daughter. Deciding that the child's freedom to choose is more important than her well-being, he releases her hand so she can cross whenever she pleases. She ventures out and is immediately struck by a car and killed. Is protecting a child's free will more important than protecting her life? Which is worth more to a father? To a child? To a loving God?

Some religions say God doesn't send anyone to hell, but that we send ourselves. This is a distinction without a difference, and yields the same revolting outcome. Though not directly engaged in the torture of his creatures, he has designed a scenario in which it takes place forever—even though he has the power to fix it.

What could anyone do to deserve such horrific treatment? When a man engages in irrationally punitive behavior of those entrusted to his care, he is tried as a criminal. We strive to correct his vile behavior because it is damaging to others. Oddly, many people expect far worse from the God they worship.

We ascribe human behaviors and attributes to things we don't understand, because humanity is all we know. We identify with a vengeful God because we are vengeful people. If such a perverse concept of God represents the moral compass guiding the religions of the world, is it any wonder that people commit the atrocities they do? Throughout history—from the Salem witch trials to the Ku Klux Klan, from the Holocaust to modern suicide bombers, from the Inquisition to slavery, from torturing fellow humans to beheading them for not adopting a religion—the most horrific acts are committed in God's name.

It has been said that men never do evil so completely and cheerfully as when they do it from religious conviction.[6] Perhaps God could do without all the help from his most zealous fans.

Humans seek to emulate the deity they worship. Our perception of this deity, whether right or wrong, has a profound impact on how we treat others. Many worship a god that behaves in ways we incarcerate men for—yet, unlike a mere man, this deity has the power and desire to inflict pain *forever*.

Is it possible that they're wrong?

RELIGION GETS IT WRONG... A LOT

Most religious groups value preserving their traditions over seeking the truth. This yields them incapable of any significant course correction, even in the face of reality. Strangely enough, this is by design. Most new groups are formed because of a disagreement. The Protestant church, for example, was established to reject the teachings of the Catholic church. Now countless factions exist within both. Like a giant tree, each branch split from an original group to form its own, over and over.

That is why so many different groups exist today. Each division was based on some defining issue, be it as petty as what women should wear, or as fundamental as which writings were divinely inspired. And each new group set forth a doctrinal statement to differentiate its beliefs from the others. This explains the multitude of divisions and internal schisms within religions.

This principle applies equally to all belief systems. Consider agnostics (who neither believe nor disbelieve in a deity, as it is unknown or cannot be known); atheists (who maintain that no deity exists); and Satanists (of which there are many different theologies). Each group has rejected the views of others, and in doing so, has formed a unique belief system of its own. Every one of them amounts to an organized religion, complete with rabid defenders preaching nuanced dogma.

A group's beliefs are predicated on disagreement with others. And the leaders of the movement have spent decades teaching their version to followers. So how would you expect a religious group's leadership to deal with new facts and enlightenment?

The answer can be found in a prime example from the United States. The Southern Baptist Convention, a Christian denomination, was established in 1845 due to disagreements with other Baptists about slavery—they *supported* it. How long did it take for the SBC to officially renounce its racist past? A century and a half![7] Shouldn't believers in God have been the first people to oppose slavery, rather than the last? The Bible on which the Southern Baptist religion was based admonishes man to love his neighbor like himself and take care of the poor.

When racism, slavery, torture, murder, or any other deplorable activity can be rationalized by pointing to a Tanakh, Bible, or Koran, we face a serious problem. Who is comfortable entrusting their fate to a deity that condones violence and hatred?

The collective conscience of humanity is offended by such acts of brutality. Why, then, are religious zealots and fundamentalists the most ardent proponents of violence against other people who were created in God's image?

Because they believe in a merciless God.

WHEN FACTS ATTACK

Some Christians teach that the entire universe and all that is in it came into existence less than ten thousand years ago. This is sometimes referred to as Young Earth Creationism. It is based

20

on a literal interpretation of the story of creation in the book of Genesis, as well as an estimated timeline drawn from biblical genealogy. However well intended, this belief appears to violate observable reality.

Radiometric dating evaluates levels of radioactive isotopes and the materials they decay into over time. While it does not offer precise measurement, it appears to date numerous artifacts at well over ten thousand years old. But even without these tests, the Young Earth theory has obvious flaws.

The speed of light is 186,000 miles per second—over 670 million miles per hour. The sun is the closest star to Earth. However, because it is so far away (about 93 million miles), it takes a while for its light to travel to us. The light we see took about 8 minutes and 19 seconds to get here. Obviously the sun had to exist eight minutes ago, or else we wouldn't see it now. Therefore, we can conclude that the sun is at least 8 minutes old.

Ursa Major is one of the more well-known constellations. Within it there are thirty-four observable galaxies. The Messier 81 galaxy lies 11.8 million light-years away from Earth. So the observable light shining from its stars took about twelve million years to travel here. Therefore, we are forced to conclude that these stars existed 11.8 million years ago.

This single galaxy alone disproves the Young Earth theory. But there are many observable light sources that are millions of light-years away. Some are even *billions* of light-years away. If the Young Earth theory were true, all stars visible from Earth would be less than ten thousand light-years away.

That is obviously not the case.

Of course, it is possible that modern science is incorrect in its understanding of how far away these galaxies really are, or how quickly light traveled through space and time at their inception. But given the evidence available to us today, we must conclude that the Young Earth hypothesis is incorrect.

Each of us must embark on a journey to find the truth ourselves. We can't expect religion to find all the answers for us.

THE CHOICE IS YOURS—OR IS IT?

Our place of birth plays a significant role in the religious beliefs we will likely choose as an adult.

- If you were born in the United States, there is a 75 percent chance you consider yourself a Christian.

- If you're from Cambodia, there's a 96 percent chance you are Buddhist.

- If you were born in Israel, odds are 75 percent that you are Jewish.

- Are you from Turkey? There's more than a 99 percent chance you are Muslim.

- If you were born in Japan, it's 84 percent likely you practice Shinto.

- Born in Nepal? There is an 81 percent chance that you are Hindu.[8]

You may have thought that people freely choose their own beliefs, but it seems more likely that their country does. Some nations even go to great lengths to promote a specific religion or stifle the flow of information about others.

WHO IS RIGHT?

There are many different religions, each divided into various sects or denominations. World religions cover a broad spectrum of ideas, but each one shares a common thread: Generally speaking, every belief system denies all the others. Each religion claims it is the only path to paradise, enlightenment, or rebirth—or that there is no afterlife at all. Each religion claims to be true, and insists that the others are wrong.

Each belief system offers its own answers for how the universe came to be, how humanity arrived on the scene, and what may lie ahead. But since there is only one reality, only one of these explanations could be right—if any.

Imagine one thousand people randomly draw one ticket each, and the person who draws ticket number 1,000 wins a cash prize. The person who drew #999 may seem close to winning, but he's just as far off as number 1. Both are losers.

The same is true of religion. If a thousand belief systems exist, and each denies the others, then only one could be right—and all the others must be wrong. If the total number of unique beliefs is one million, then 999,999 have to be wrong.[9]

While we cannot deny that there is only one truth, we may be wrong about our version of it. The odds are certainly not in our favor. That's why it's important not to force our beliefs on others.

We must give each other the freedom to discover the truth on our own, especially in light of all the misinformation that exists, how long it takes to sort through it all, and the enormous pressure to embrace a prevalent belief in one's culture. If a belief could be spread by force, it would have already. The truth need not be forced on anyone; it will reveal itself in time.

The truth remains true, whether we have discovered it or not.

TOUGH QUESTIONS

No religion has all the answers, of course. For instance, although it is the most widespread faith in the world, even mainstream Christianity presents many problems and contradictions:

- If a good person doesn't accept Christ before he dies, will God really send him to be tormented in endless hell?

- What will God do with good people who were led into a

religion that is not the "right" one? Will they be separated from God forever, along with evil people?

- If God knew beforehand that certain people would go to hell, why create them in the first place? Why not spare them the misery of existing at all?

- What happens to all the people who existed before Jesus walked the earth two thousand years ago? Biblical icons such as Moses, Noah, and David were all born before him, and did not know his name. Are they in hell?

- If a relationship with Jesus is the only way to heaven, do infants and the mentally disabled go to hell when they die?

Generations of theologians, pastors, and priests have wrestled with questions like these. When asked, many will give boilerplate answers such as "We just have to trust in God's righteousness," or "There are just some things we may never understand."

This is deeply troubling. Do they really expect people to stake it all on answers like that?

CHAPTER 4

CAUSE

*The notion that science and spirituality are somehow
mutually exclusive does a disservice to both.*

— CARL SAGAN

Y OU EXIST. If you are the effect, what was the cause? Are you
the result of random chance, or did someone put you here?
Maybe our existence is just a fluke. Perhaps we are the product
of natural selection through evolution. But do these hypotheses
adequately explain the precise order found in the cosmos?

How can a universe subject to the unbreakable laws of physics
simultaneously be random? How was the extraordinarily delicate
balance between order and chance calibrated so perfectly as to
produce such an astounding level of organization?

Imagine yourself hiking down a forest trail, surrounded on all
sides by pristine natural beauty. As you make your way through
the wilderness, your eye is drawn off the path and into the woods.
You notice that each tree is in a row, equally spaced apart from the
others. *This is unnatural,* you think. *Someone planted those trees
in perfect lines.* It is easy to distinguish between planned order
and random chance.

That evening, as you turn on the news, the reporter describes a fascinating find. Shocking high-resolution photos sent back from an exploration spacecraft dispatched to the surface of Mars reveal images of what is unmistakably a metal spatula. How can this be? Perhaps it's just a naturally occurring spatula. Given enough time and randomness, surely a similar utensil would spontaneously appear *somewhere* in the universe, right?

Of course not. Apart from intelligent beings, it is impossible to explain how such an item got there.

A spatula is not a complex machine. There are no interconnected parts, no chemical reactions. But we know—without a doubt—that someone had to have constructed it. And yet, when we look at something infinitely more complex, such as a worm or a tree, some casually dismiss it as ordinary. Indeed, many of us were taught that our bodies are the product of time and chance.

Why does such a double standard exist? The underlying reason is that some people believe our universe was created, while others disagree. Which is true? Neither possibility can be definitively proven. Many people believe as they do simply because the alternative is undesirable. However, emotion rarely leads to a logical conclusion. We must consider the facts.

Those who believe in a creator often advance the *teleological* argument, or the idea that nature has order by design. It has been proposed throughout history by great thinkers such as Socrates, Plato, Aristotle, Cicero, and Thomas Aquinas, often using similar analogies such as the discovery of a watch or timepiece. It deducts that the world around us must have had a cause. This reasoning has led many people to conclude that something or someone must have designed our earth and its inhabitants.

Others believe that infinite possibilities will ultimately result in something remarkable—even something as orderly and complex as our universe. Some use the analogy that given enough time, an infinite number of monkeys seated in front of an infinite number of typewriters could generate the complete works of Shakespeare. An experiment carried out at Paignton Zoo in England tested a group of six monkeys' progress at this goal. Researchers were left with little more than a few pages repeating the letter *S* and a broken computer that had been urinated and defecated on.[1]

Maybe the monkeys just needed more time. Or maybe there weren't enough monkeys on the job.

This theory raises a critical question: Where would all these monkeys and typewriters come from in the first place? Both the monkey and the typewriter are incredibly complex. They couldn't appear out of thin air. That would violate the laws of nature. It would be unnatural... *super*natural.

Even if we were to accept that these two items *did* inexplicably materialize within an infinitely large universe, what are the odds that a typewriter would appear right in front of a monkey? There are simply too many requirements that can only be the product of careful planning.

The best theories science has to offer fail to answer the vital questions of life. Where did all this order come from? How did matter come to exist? What established the laws of physics that govern our world? Why is life only found on Earth? There is no explanation based on random chance that can sufficiently address these quandaries. Our universe demonstrates order so absolute that we can employ the scientific method with certainty to test our theories. Order allows the trajectory of a spacecraft to be calculated with precision. Order allows us to accurately measure the speeds of sound and light. Order gives us the means to find the exact distance between our planet and a faraway galaxy.

If adding two numbers produced a random result each time, we could never rely on math. Fortunately there are definite answers with no variation. Similarly, there is nothing random about the study of science. If each iteration of an experiment yielded a different result from the same variables, we would not be able to conclude anything with certainty. The scientific method is not compatible with randomness. If the universe were truly random, the study of science itself would not be possible.

The laws of nature stand in direct opposition to the notion that all is born of chance. The difficulty this presents for scientists is eloquently summed up by mathematician Steven Strogatz:

> Scientists have often been baffled by the existence of spontaneous order in the universe. The laws of thermodynamics seem to dictate the opposite, that nature should inexorably degenerate toward a state of greater disorder, greater entropy. Yet all around us we see magnificent structures—galaxies, cells, ecosystems, human beings—that have all somehow managed to assemble themselves. This enigma bedevils all of science today.[2]

There is no sufficient scientific explanation for the orderly world we live in. And every theory ever advanced to explain the origin of the universe is pure conjecture, because no one was present to witness the beginning of time, space, matter, or life. But there are some facts science has made clear beyond question.

TURTLES AND PHYSICS

There's an old tale of an Eastern guru who, when asked what holds the world in place, replies that the earth rests upon the back of a tiger. When asked what holds the tiger up, he answers that the tiger stands upon an elephant. When asked what holds up the elephant, he replies that it rests on the back of a turtle. When asked what the turtle stands on, the old teacher pauses for just a moment, then says, "Why, it's turtles all the way down!"

His answer is similar to an argument often made against the existence of a god: *If God exists, who created him?* The implication, of course, is that the creator itself would need to be created. This seems sensible in the context of physics. However, a deity is a supernatural being—beyond the natural—which, by definition, is not subject to the laws of nature. A deity may choose to impose laws upon the material universe it creates, but those laws would not constrain the deity. A "supreme" being that can't defy nature would certainly be less than supreme.

Turtles, on the other hand, are physical beings, subject to the laws of nature. Same with a rock. And a tree. And our universe. And people. All these tangible things exist within the corporeal realm. Therefore, their presence necessitates explanation.

If a supreme deity exists, it would be the *primum movens* or "first cause" that originated all that is presently observed within the physical realm. A deity is not defined as a creation, but a creator. It is not an effect, but rather a cause—the first cause.

Science, by definition, does not deal with the supernatural: its disciplines are limited only to the observable physical world. The sciences provide a wealth of knowledge and insight, but only into the natural. As a result, it is impossible for science to either prove or refute the existence of God, but it does offer clues.

So, what has science concluded regarding the history of the natural universe?

A HUGE DISRUPTION

In 1916, Albert Einstein published his general theory of relativity. His work has proved essential in understanding the effects of gravitational attraction. He spent a significant amount of time studying other theories and considering multiple possibilities before he released his findings.

Nevertheless, shortly after unleashing general relativity on the scientific community, Einstein made a slight modification to it. He determined from his own equations that the universe must be either expanding or contracting—and he was not comfortable with either possibility. To support his preferred notion that the universe was static, he added a "cosmological constant" to his general theory of relativity. In doing so, he was able to prevent the universe from contracting until it collapsed or expanding into oblivion... at least on paper.

In the 1920s, Edwin Hubble discovered that our Milky Way galaxy is not the only one in the universe. He found many more. But Hubble's studies of these newfound galaxies revealed something shocking: they were all moving away from us and from one another. The universe is not constant. Einstein was wrong.

Though groundbreaking, the premise behind Hubble's novel discovery was simple. Have you ever stood still while a police car or ambulance passed by with sirens blaring? The pitch of the siren seems to get higher as the vehicle approaches and lower after it passes. This is called the Doppler effect. The pitch of the siren stays the same, but the vehicle's movement produces sound with a higher or lower pitch for the stationary observer.

This is what Hubble noticed throughout the universe. Instead of listening for sounds, though, he studied the color of the light emitted by faraway stars and galaxies. These light sources always displayed an increased wavelength, or a "redder" shade. The light he observed from distant galaxies was shifted toward the red end of the spectrum since every observable light source was moving away. This measured effect is called *redshift*, which formed the basis for Hubble's data. His observations over the years culminated in Hubble's Law, which demonstrates that the universe is not constant, but is in fact expanding.

Then, in 2011, the Nobel Prize in Physics was awarded to three researchers for their 1998 discovery of "the accelerating expansion of the universe through observations of distant supernovae."[3] The team observed that our universe isn't merely expanding, but that its expansion is *accelerating*. In other words, everything in the universe appears to be flying apart at increasing speed.

Imagine a slow-motion video of a watermelon being smashed with a sledgehammer. If you played the clip backward, you would first see messy watermelon bits everywhere, maybe even on the camera lens. As the footage played backward, the tiny pieces would collect, clump together, move closer to a common point, and finally pull together to form a perfect watermelon.

If everything is moving farther apart as time goes on, then everything must have been closer together in the past. Imagine viewing footage from a cosmological surveillance camera that has been filming since the very beginning of the universe. Rolling the video backward, you would see all the mass in the universe gravitate inward, clump together, and draw tightly into one single point, just like the watermelon.

Given the laws of physics, our universe appears to be expanding from some central point of origin. If we could rewind history, we would witness a finite point from which space and time began. This is why the Big Bang theory is currently the most widely accepted model to describe the origin of the universe.

At the time the Big Bang theory began to gain traction, many cosmologists still preferred a steady-state universe that remained unchanged, much like the one Einstein envisioned. Perhaps some did not care for the apparent theological implications a Big Bang would present, since it points directly to a universe that was born *ex nihilo*—out of nothing. Yet science makes it clear that mass can neither be created nor destroyed, as this would violate principles of conservation. Simply put, science points to an event that it assures us could not possibly have occurred.

Physicists concede that the laws of nature do not explain the moments leading up to or immediately following the Big Bang. Laws of physics would have to be violated in order for time, mass, and energy to come into existence where they did not exist before.

Science admits this took place, but it can't explain how.

New discoveries continue to support the Big Bang model, yet they raise more questions about a universe born from nothing. Some people resist this new information because it threatens their personal belief systems. They prefer to believe that no creator exists. To avoid the theological implications of this inexplicable event, some have proffered various cosmological models that describe parallel universes, an oscillating universe, and many other convoluted ideas. These more complex hypotheses contend that an occurrence such as the Big Bang may not be so rare. They aim to increase the odds of spontaneously creating the universe we see around us, just as more monkeys and typewriters would allow more opportunities to produce a literary masterpiece.

Whether the universe is static or oscillating, would these ideas sufficiently explain its origin? No. If ours were one of many parallel universes, would we finally know how time began? No. If a "multiverse" existed, would that explain where all the matter in it came from? No. Such conjecture only raises more questions.

All of this violates the commonsense logic of Occam's Razor, a guiding principle that favors the most economic explanation of any phenomenon. Scientists call it *lex parsimoniae*, a Latin expression directing us to choose the explanation that makes the fewest assumptions. Yet sometimes they themselves do not.[4]

In his book *The Grand Design*, physicist Stephen Hawking wrote, "Because there is a law like gravity, the universe can and will create itself from nothing."[5] Yet Hawking failed to address where "a law like gravity" came from in the first place. Why did it need to exist without matter on which to act? Who authored this unnecessary law? Are we to believe that randomness resulted in these inviolable laws of order? If so, who created the chaos, or the fixed tendency for order to emerge from it?

Tellingly, Hawking also once stated, "One can't prove that God doesn't exist, but science makes God unnecessary."[6] Why do some individuals spend an inordinate amount of time carefully crafting positions designed to eliminate the inescapable necessity for a first cause? Is there an underlying aversion to theism that shapes these perceptions? Did Einstein choose to see our universe as constant for a similar reason? Brilliant as he was, he was wrong. He regretted adding the cosmological constant to avoid expansion or contraction.[7] Einstein had initially been correct, but he attempted to bend his findings to meet his own preconceived notions. He, of all people, should have known better: science has no concern for our preferences. Our conclusions must be based on observable reality.

A true logician would not allow his personal beliefs to hinder objective research. Yet some attempt to dazzle us with wild ideas that amount to little more than pseudoscience. These concepts demand more blind faith than the theological implications they seek to supplant. Most of us aren't as adept at practicing such skillful cognitive dissonance, and we must embrace the obvious truth: something cannot come from nothing. The natural laws which govern our universe demand that every physical effect have a root cause. Our world had to have a first cause.

The only tenable explanation is that a supernatural force—an outside force not bound by the laws of nature—created time, space, and all matter. Yes, this theory lies outside the realm of science and cannot be proven, but the laws of physics point inescapably to this conclusion.

HIGHLY CALIBRATED

Our galaxy, the Milky Way, has been estimated to contain up to fifty billion planets like those found in our own solar system. This massive figure covers only a tiny portion of the cosmos. Scientists have observed a staggeringly large expanse populated with trillions and trillions of stars, each potentially with its own solar system of planets.

Some researchers downplay the rarity of life, suggesting that it may be far more common than once thought. But why don't we see evidence of it anywhere else? Physicist Enrico Fermi once asked this question, which became known as Fermi's Paradox.

In order to support life a planet must occupy a habitable zone, a region defined by both its planetary system and the galaxy in which that system lies. Both must be hospitable. This rules out planets that are too close or too far from stars, with extremes of temperature or gravity. Other conditions that determine whether a planet can support life and sustain metabolism include atmosphere, composition, and water presence.[8]

A large array of variables must be within a narrow band of perfectly tuned values in order for a planet to be hospitable to life. Not *most* of these requirements, but *all* of them must be met in order for life to exist.[9] Even with all the other necessities in place, Earth could not host life without oxygen or water. Life cannot exist with a level of gravity that is too high or too low. Or on a planet whose axis tilts just a little too far away from its sun during winter, or too close during summer.

Maybe that's why we have yet to see any evidence of life, past or present, elsewhere in the universe. There is only one green-and-blue planet teeming with life. It seems we *are* special. Maybe we have been given a sky full of lifeless stars and planets simply so we would realize how rare life is—and how unique we are.

TINY MACHINES

A fevered search is underway for other life forms in outer space. But if single-celled organisms could be found on a remote planet, would that explain their origin, or how they arrived there? Would it prove that a creator does not exist? No. Life, wherever it is found and in whatever form, demands explanation.

The culmination of mankind's innovations over the entire span of history is technology. Perhaps the most fundamental building block of our recent advances is the electronic circuit. From communication to health, from productivity to manufacturing, from research to design, the computer has dramatically changed life as we know it. The irony is that in our quest to design the most advanced technology possible, we have created something that roughly resembles one of our body's own cells—though far less complex, powerful, or efficient.

Life at a cellular level is comprised of cells and DNA. Scientists have compared the cell to an organic computer, and DNA as its software.[10] Each base pair in a DNA double helix can be expressed as one of four values. This makes genetic code essentially a digital program. The DNA software tells the cellular hardware which proteins should be created and in what sequence.

A computer can't function without code to execute, and code is useless without a computer to run it on. Each part is required. The same is true of life: both a cell *and* some genetic code are required. A cell can't function without the code, and DNA does nothing unless a cell reads it.

Code doesn't create computers, and computers don't create their own code.[11] Someone must design and create both of these components specifically to operate with each other. All living organisms must be preloaded with genetic code, without which they cannot possibly survive or replicate.

Theories of evolution fail to explain how this requirement was first satisfied. Natural selection requires a functional cell, complete with genetic code, to replicate itself continuously in order to bring about favorable mutations or adaptations. Natural selection will never explain the *origin* of life because, by definition, life must already exist for natural selection to occur. Evolutionary theory only attempts to address changes that take place *after* life began. It starts in the middle, with perfectly functional life forms already loaded with precise genetic code.

Cells require genetic code to function. Lots of it. The genetic code in our DNA is extremely complex. The human genome contains roughly three billion base pairs, which is enough data to consume about 750 megabytes. And this code is not merely a string of random values: within it are countless precise instructions such as a start codon, an amino acid sequence, and a stop codon to synthesize the necessary proteins—a perfect algorithm for life and reproduction.

Feeding random data into a computer as if it were code and then trying to execute it will do nothing other than crash it. For a computer to work, the instructions it executes must follow exact specifications, carefully crafted to generate the desired outcome.

In the same way, DNA requires a specific set of instructions in order to produce a functional life form. Human-to-human genetic differences account for a mere 0.5 percent in variation from one person to the next. As different as we may appear from one another, this is not much variation. Even a fruit fly shares an estimated 60 percent of its genetic code with humans.[12] The code of life is certainly not random. It is so precise that even minor mutations can result in genetic disorders that stunt or end life.

This is where our analogy must end, because a cell is far more impressive than any electronic circuit. Even our most powerful computers do not approach the awe-inspiring complexity of a single living cell. Yet there is another feat that sets the cell apart: Unlike any device ever created, it can preserve and replicate itself without any help. A cell's structure and genetic code allow it to divide and multiply endlessly, creating more identical hardware and software. Even if we were to design a computer system that could achieve a similar result, there would be no doubt that it was the product of engineering genius.

The energy of life originally imparted to a cell is a mystery. Once the last cell of its type dies, it is gone forever. We are unable to animate cells, or even bring dead ones back to life. We're relegated to researching remnants of the original spark of life once breathed into living things. Science, presently consumed by a quest to alter the genetic code these cells run, comes nowhere close to creating life, or even explaining its origin.

Despite the organization visible in our world today, entropy is taking hold. Order is winding down. The environment is becoming more polluted. Genetic mutations are yielding less healthy outcomes: more cancer, more autism, more disease. Studies suggest that modern man may have lower body mass, a less robust skeleton, smaller brain size, and weaker teeth than some of our ancestors.[13]

These trends continue, despite recent advances in nutrition and medicine. Contrary to what many of us were taught, humans do not appear to be evolving into something superior. Rather, we seem to be devolving into weaker, more fragile creatures as physical, mental, behavioral, and learning disorders compound upon each new generation. It's as though we've made hundreds of photocopies of the original DNA, and with each pass we lose a little more fidelity from our once-pristine genetic code. We are not adding enhanced features through natural selection; instead we are decaying rapidly.

The ideas advanced by modern scientific research to explain the origin of life are primarily focused on a concept called *abiogenesis*, which is defined as the process of life emerging from lifeless matter—something that has never been witnessed. These hypotheses begin with conditions favorable to life (like a puddle of primordial ooze rich with organic matter and a suitable atmosphere) from which a single-celled organism manages to construct itself.

This amounts to nothing but wild speculation.

Science has demonstrated conclusively that life cannot materialize from lifeless matter. If that were possible, surely myriad forms of life—or their remains—would be scattered across the cosmos. Yet we've never discovered a single living cell anywhere other than on Earth.

Life does not routinely spring up out of nowhere. If this had taken place in the past, why don't we still see it happening? We are told, conveniently, that conditions for life to spontaneously emerge were much more favorable back then than they are now.

Though creative, these concepts fail to explain how the organic matter came to be in the first place, or how it became increasingly more complex, formed a cell, loaded itself with genetic code, and then came alive when conditions were just right.

Setting aside the mechanics of this series of divine miracles, there are clearly no better conditions for life in the universe than what our planet has to offer today. Look at all the varied forms of life it is home to. A snail is a basic model of functional cells with genetic code. It has well-developed organs to help it survive. But if it dies, no amount of lightning, radiation, sunlight, electricity, or any other form of energy imaginable could give even an existing, prebuilt organism its life back.

The odds of a single-celled organism spontaneously emerging from a swamp of protein-rich primordial ooze are not good. All observable evidence points to zero. Even if this were possible, we would still have no explanation for where the ooze itself came from. How, then, are we supposed to believe that life cropped up out of nothing but lifeless matter, without any assistance at all?

In light of the evidence, the idea of macroevolution is a leap of faith most logical people will find very difficult to accept.

A HIGHER POWER

The laws of nature dictate that the universe could never emerge from nothing, and life could never emerge from lifeless matter. Essentially, science indicates we should not exist—yet we do.

Some people reject the concept of a creator on the grounds that we lack hard proof of its existence. Just as there is no tenable scientific explanation to address how matter came to exist, there is no explanation for the spirit of life that animates us.

There can never be scientifically demonstrable proof that God exists because the supernatural lies outside the realm of science. Conversely, there's no way to prove that God *doesn't* exist. As astronomer, cosmologist, and astrophysicist Carl Sagan observed,

"An atheist has to know a lot more than I know. An atheist is someone who knows there is no god. By some definitions atheism is very stupid."[14]

Science leaves most of our world unexplained. Vital details of our origin remain a mystery. As we discover more about life and its miraculous inner workings, it seems a supernatural first cause requires far less faith than the alternative. A creator is the only plausible explanation behind our precision-tuned universe and the rare life in it.

Virtually everyone agrees that a higher power exists. A May 2011 Gallup poll revealed that more than nine in ten Americans say they believe in God.[15] Though there are many different takes on what that god may be like, the vast majority believe that one exists. On what do these people base their belief? Is there some kind of evidence hiding in plain sight?

Our planet has been host to innumerable tribes, cultures, and groups of humanity, many of them isolated and without means of communication. Nevertheless, humans share an astounding number of innate traits—characteristics that seem more spiritual than genetic. These similarities suggest humans have been designed to appreciate and understand common abstract concepts.

When sad or angry, all people cry or frown. When happy, we laugh and smile. This is not a learned or cultural phenomenon. But why are we happy? Why do we laugh? What defines humor?

All of us take pleasure in music. Though tastes in styles differ greatly, everyone appreciates some type of musical composition. Why is music so universally appealing? What makes us able to detect when it is off-key? Why does it so often make us move and sway and dance? Why do we sing to our children?

Humans love to communicate. For thousands of years we have told tales, recorded events, and passed on oral traditions. Usually our stories lead us to root for the underdog or the good guy. Why do we want the forces of good to prevail over evil? Why do we like happy endings? Why are we disappointed when circumstances don't turn out the way we hoped?

What makes us so keenly aware of the golden rule? Every one of us has a sense of right and wrong that makes us feel slighted when someone treats us unfairly. Why does everyone seem to have the same basic expectations when it comes to what is fair?

Is it possible that we were created by a higher power, who gave us an innate sense of and appreciation for universal truths? Is it possible that we were created to think like our creator?

Believers in a higher power, a supernatural being, or a grand designer may differ on specifics, but virtually all of humanity has come to realize that all people share a common identity. Mankind has spent a considerable amount of time reflecting on this sense of shared spirit and purpose. It is evident in our works of art, our traditions, our values, our lives. We seek to honor something greater than ourselves—a creator we have yet to fully understand. Long before science confirmed how miraculous our existence is, common sense pointed to the same conclusion: *We were designed.*

So, why are we here? Would the creator just set the universe in motion and leave it to play out on its own?

Or would he reach out to us?

CHAPTER 5

MESSAGE

*What comes into our minds when we think about God
is the most important thing about us.*

— A. W. TOZER

THE MAJORITY of people, past and present, have concluded that a higher power exists. From this common starting point, however, the possibilities diverge in all directions: Is our creator an impersonal god who merely created a cosmic ant farm? Is he concerned with our daily struggles? Has he contacted us? These are the questions that various belief systems purport to answer, and this is where it gets quite interesting.

Even though there are a multitude of religions—and also many denominations within each one—there is a clear consensus among many on certain points. Some of the fundamental beliefs shared by the most prevalent religions are remarkably consistent, at least with regard to the identity of the creator.

Most people believe there is one supernatural creator. This is called *monotheism*. However, this is not the only type of theism represented by world religions. Some worship multiple deities, which is *polytheism*. And some believe that the matter in the universe is itself divine—a form of *pantheism*. Yet the number of people who believe in these other ways pales in comparison to the majority view that a single God exists.

If anyone can invent any religion based on any type of deity (or deities) imaginable, then what makes one all-powerful God the norm? Why is monotheism so prevalent today, especially when many ancient writings and cultures describe multiple gods?

IN A WORD

Since time travel isn't possible, modern knowledge about ancient cultures and world history is based largely on old writings.

Homer's *Iliad* is one of the oldest and most popular works of literature ever recorded. Scholars estimate that this epic Greek poem, which likely originated as an oral tradition, was first put in writing around 800 BC. The oldest full copy of *Iliad* we have is likely the Venetus A manuscript, which was carefully written by hand on papyrus—paper made from a reed that grows in Egypt. Dated circa AD 900, this 1,100-year-old document is the oldest complete *extant manuscript* (surviving copy) we have found.

Documents handwritten on papyrus tend not to last long, so skilled copiers called *scribes* often made new copies to preserve them. Some of the oldest fragments of *Iliad* we have found (such as Papyrus Oxyrhynchus 21) date back to about AD 100. Though not complete copies, these older fragments can be compared with newer versions to confirm that the text has stayed true to the original throughout years of duplication. Scholars are able to evaluate these additional sources to detect and correct any transcription errors in a process known as *textual criticism*.

Most of our ancient literature is based on just a handful of manuscripts—often less than ten. Even a few can confirm the text's reliability. But Homer's *Iliad* is remarkable: archaeologists have found at least 704 published papyri of it.[1] Such an unusually high number of sources indicates that it was quite popular.

Compare this to the greatest work by the Roman historian Tacitus: The *Annals* is a vital source of information about the Roman Empire. Our version of the text is based on only 27 manuscripts—several hundred less than *Iliad*. Despite this, most scholars are confident this work has reached us intact.

Imagine what textual critics must think when they compare the Bible to other ancient works. The Bible is divided into two halves: the Old Testament in Hebrew, and the New Testament in Greek. The New Testament alone has over 5,800 Greek manuscripts, plus about 10,000 Latin manuscripts, and over 9,300 manuscripts in various other translations. With over 25,000 manuscripts available, scholars have more sources than any other document ever recorded to compare and cross-check for reliability. New Testament manuscripts provide over one thousand times more source material than the vast majority of literature we rely on to derive our knowledge of ancient culture and history.

While the number of manuscripts is an excellent indicator of popularity and overall influence, the existence of tens of thousands of copies does not mean a work is free of transmission errors. Textual critics also closely examine the time difference between the moment a work was first penned and its oldest copy. The sooner a copy was created after the original, the more reliable it is presumed to be. In the case of *Iliad*, the oldest copy we have was made about 1,700 years after the original. That leaves a considerable amount of time for errors to have crept in. Tacitus' *Annals* yields a far smaller gap of about 1,000 years, which is much better. But the oldest New Testament manuscripts were produced within just 250 years of the original document, and in some instances, less than a hundred. This is substantially less than other writings that experts rely on to understand world history.

The Old Testament survived a tumultuous history in the care of Jewish leaders, and still we have hundreds of manuscripts. Recent discoveries such as the Dead Sea Scrolls in 1947 have unearthed thousands of fragments of Old Testament texts, pushing our earliest copies back one thousand years closer to the original.

When compared to newer manuscripts, these early copies reveal centuries of precise transmission, unlike any other work of ancient literature. The integrity of the text has been attributed to the extreme care taken by Jewish scribes to preserve their sacred writings. These scribes, called the guardians of the text, were specially trained to count the total letters in each section, locate and verify the center letter and center words, and destroy all copies that contained errors. They calculated the ancient equivalent of a digital checksum for each copy, and eliminated those that failed the test.

So, what does all this mean? First, it becomes immediately clear to the objective critic that if we are going to reject the Bible as unreliably transmitted, then every other ancient text we rely on must also be tossed out. It is by far the most dependable ancient work ever preserved. While some may disagree with the message it contains, the Bible's text has assuredly reached us intact.

Second, the Bible has proven to be the most popular and most replicated literary work in history. But why this book? Humanity's unparalleled devotion to preserving this particular document cannot simply be dismissed.

For these reasons, among all the possible accounts of mankind's origins, the Bible is likely to have pertinent information. After all, it contains the most prevalent and most widely disseminated explanation ever recorded.

A UNIQUE WORK

The popularity of the Bible is undeniable, but that alone proves nothing. We must examine what, if anything, sets it apart.

The Bible has had an immeasurable impact on the cultures and beliefs of the world. Whether or not you would give credence to the religious views expressed by its authors, there is no doubt that it offers immense literary value to scholars. It is a treasure trove of history, genealogy, and geography that has greatly informed our understanding of the past.

But the Bible goes much further than merely representing itself as an account of history: it purports to answer questions regarding the origin and purpose of mankind, as well as the identity of the creator. These are big claims.

The word "Bible" comes from the Koine Greek phrase *ta biblia*, which simply means "the books." It is a collection of writings from various authors whose works were preserved separately by different groups for many centuries. Those who protected and studied these various writings believed the original authors were inspired by the creator of the universe, so they carefully replicated and guarded them. In time, these individual works began to be grouped together. Eventually a list of 66 books—all believed to have been divinely inspired—was agreed upon to standardize the collection. This final list is called the *canon*, and its compilation forms the modern Bible.[2]

Of course, other works have also asserted divine origins. The Book of Mormon is a fascinating example, and the circumstances surrounding its creation should give any objective critic pause. It was written around 1830 exclusively by Joseph Smith, a treasure hunter who said he was visited on a hill near his home by angels who gave him golden plates with hieroglyphics on them. Eleven witnesses signed statements indicating they saw the golden plates, though some later recanted.

The translations of these plates were purportedly "seen" by Mr. Smith by peering into a magic stone placed inside a top hat, and then spoken aloud for a friend to transcribe. Mr. Smith claimed to receive many personal revelations from God—revelations that no one else witnessed—which are central to the Mormon faith. Among them were instructions to engage in polygamy and take many brides, which Mr. Smith did. He had at least thirty-three wives, some as young as fourteen years of age.[3] Original church beliefs, recorded in *Doctrine and Covenants* 132, teach that men who do not engage in polygamy will be damned, and those who do will become gods. The modern Mormon church, which calls itself "The Church of Jesus Christ of Latter-day Saints," has struggled internally with this strange teaching for decades.[4]

Today, the Mormon church publicly denounces polygamy, even though it is explicitly endorsed in writings they claim were divinely inspired. If it were truly a revelation from God directly to the founder of Mormonism, why not defend it? Surely they wouldn't invalidate a commandment from God simply because it became unpopular. In reality, the Mormon church's rejection of Smith's purported revelation is a tacit admission that their prophet's message from God was false. This should call into question *all* of his teachings, instead of just those that rewarded him with multiple young wives. Perhaps Joseph Smith was not a prophet at all, but an imaginative leader with a personal agenda.

The religious text of Islam is based on visions of an angel named Gabriel which began around AD 609. These events took place inside a cave, with only one witness. Muhammad described his revelations to others, and they were repeated, memorized, and transcribed over many years to ultimately form the Koran.

It is not unheard of for men to report seeing visions or angels. There are similar events described in the Bible. But difficulty arises when game-changing revelations are given only to a single person. Without witnesses, prophecy, or miracles to confirm their authenticity, how will others know? Such circumstances warrant strong skepticism. The creator is unlikely to reveal himself in such secretive ways.

Each self-proclaimed prophet emerges with a new take on life or a novel approach to spirituality, and people are automatically suspicious. But we should be *extremely* cautious when teachings promote personal power, influence, or material prosperity. Any religions that advance wealth, political ascension, superiority, control, violence, or sexual gratification at the expense of others stand completely at odds with a benevolent deity.

The Bible remains the *de facto* standard against which all other religious works are contrasted. Each that has followed sought to differentiate itself from biblical teachings by stating that its message supersedes, corrects, or clarifies what has been corrupted by men. Such positions are precisely what the authors of the Book of Mormon and the Koran were forced to take, since the Bible's influence cannot be ignored.

But why is the Bible revered in this way, even by those who reject it? What makes it different from other religious texts?

First, its message comes from many disparate authors rather than just one. Scholars estimate there were as many as forty contributors—most of whom never met each other—that wrote from many locations across three continents. They were also alive at different times, so the content was recorded over a period of about fifteen hundred years.

It is highly unlikely that these authors were collaborating to perpetrate a hoax. Nor were they a small, tight-knit group seeking to start a church for money, power, or recognition.

In fact, scholars are not entirely certain who authored some books of the Bible. This underscores the absence of a self-serving motive to gain fame or wealth. Those whose identities were revealed often suffered imprisonment, torture, or painful death as a result of their involvement—far from reaping the benefits of stardom. Their perseverance despite the danger and personal cost strongly suggests that the authors believed the Bible was more than merely a collection of fictional stories; they obviously thought its message was true if they were willing to die for it.

The authors' identities represent all walks of life: herdsmen, military generals, servants, physicians, tax collectors, fishermen, kings, and others. Each writer's status, education, and background shaped his contribution, so each one carries a unique style from a different time, place, and perspective. David cried out for help from God. Paul wrote while imprisoned. King Solomon wrote from the comforts of great wealth in search of true happiness. They had little in common other than their beliefs, which is perhaps the most striking point.

An *anthology* is a collection of various works. If you contacted ten authors today—all from the same country, culture, and century—and asked them to each write a brief article regarding their political beliefs, you would have ten entirely different views: an anthology. The Bible, however, uniformly and consistently addresses the most controversial topics of all, including religion, moral values, and right and wrong. Each author agrees with the others despite being separated by vast chasms of time, geography, and culture. The resulting work addresses the most hotly debated topics with striking unanimity—a virtually impossible feat, even in our modern age of communication.

Another unique quality of the Bible lies in its frank admissions of human failure. Whereas ancient historical accounts were often underwritten by political leaders to reflect superior leadership, pristine character, or the "winner's version" of history, the Bible readily exposes the flaws and fears of its subjects. The authors display candid honesty in describing unflattering events such as King David's acts of adultery and murder, rather than rewriting them for his benefit—a testament to the text's overall credibility and accuracy.

Finally, the Bible has enjoyed immense popularity, and has consequently become the focus of thousands of years of debate. Because so many other works have quoted passages from it, scholars could easily reconstruct the Bible in its entirety even if we did not have a single copy. This demonstrates the reliability of the text, the strength of its circulation, its pervasiveness in translation to numerous languages, and its continued survival despite persecution and criticism from those seeking to destroy it, such as the Roman Emperor Diocletian.

To be clear, none of this proves that the contents of the Bible are true. However, it demonstrates conclusively that it is the most unique literary work ever recorded. It is distinguished from all other books, including those that claim to have been divinely inspired. In light of these facts, it is logical to conclude that if the truth about our creator exists in a written record, then the Bible is the only suitable candidate for consideration.

If we can determine that the Bible was *not* divinely inspired, then we can safely conclude that we haven't received a message from God, since no other work rises to the level of rare qualities it possesses.

ONE STORY, MANY FOLLOWERS

The first half of the Bible contains the books of the Old Testament, which scholars believe was originally recorded between about 1400 BC and 400 BC. This part is the same as the Hebrew Bible (called the *Tanakh*) read by followers of Judaism.

The Old Testament is regarded by three of the world's most prominent religions as divinely inspired. Impossible as it may seem, Jews, Christians, and Muslims alike—despite a history of conflict and bloodshed—all agree on this point.[5]

In fact, these groups also believe the Old Testament authors were inspired by the *same God*. As different as their religions appear today, they share a common belief in both the authenticity of this work and the identity of our creator.

This may come as a surprise to those not already familiar with each of these religions. Do Muslims worship the same God as Christians? As Jews? In a sense, yes: each faith claims to worship the one true God, and each finds its roots in the story of a man named Abram found in the Old Testament.

Genesis, the first book of the Bible, describes a man named

Adam as the first human created by God. It traces his lineage down to a descendant named Abram, and then states that God appeared before Abram and made a promise to him:

> Abram fell facedown, and God said to him, "As for me, this is my covenant with you: You will be the father of many nations. No longer will you be called Abram; your name will be Abraham, for I have made you a father of many nations. I will make you very fruitful; I will make nations of you, and kings will come from you. I will establish my covenant as an everlasting covenant between me and you and your descendants after you for the generations to come, to be your God and the God of your descendants after you." (Genesis 17:3–7 NIV)

Genesis indicates that despite this promise, Abraham's wife Sarai seemed unable to bear children. After years of waiting, she finally offered her servant Hagar to Abraham so they could conceive, and his first son, Ishmael, was born. And then, fourteen years later, Abraham and Sarai finally had their promised son together, Isaac.

As predicted, Abraham's descendants were certainly fruitful: Ishmael is regarded as the father of various Arab tribes and the ancestor of Muhammad, and Isaac's son Jacob became the father of the twelve tribes of Israel—the ancestors of King David and Jesus of Nazareth. The Old Testament states that all the world would be blessed through the children of Jacob. God identifies himself to this group, called the Israelites, as "the God of your fathers, the God of Abraham, Isaac and Jacob."

The Bible then chronicles the history of the nation of Israel as they moved to Egypt due to famine, grew in number and were subsequently enslaved by Pharaoh, were led out of captivity by Moses, wandered in the desert in search of the land God had promised them, received the Mosaic laws at Mount Sinai they were to follow, and took control of the land of Canaan. When Moses first encountered God and asked his name,

> God replied to Moses, "I AM WHO I AM. Say this to the
> people of Israel: I AM has sent me to you." God also said to
> Moses, "Say this to the people of Israel: Yahweh, the God
> of your ancestors—the God of Abraham, the God of Isaac,
> and the God of Jacob—has sent me to you. This is my
> eternal name, my name to remember for all generations."
> (Exodus 3:14–15 NLT)

Some versions render the first name God gave as "I AM THAT I AM,"
and many translate the Hebrew *Yahweh* as "LORD." In any case,
the Bible depicts God as making himself known and accessible
to men—not an anonymous power over nature, but a personal
deliverer from bondage for the Israelites.

Notably, one of the laws given to Moses was that the people
of Israel were to "have no other gods before me." God alone was
to be worshiped—a clear rejection of the polytheism many had
embraced at the time. This history of Abraham and the Israelites
explains the prevalence of monotheism today. The Old Testament
states that the entire universe was created by the one true God of
Abraham, Isaac, and Jacob—the same God who revealed himself
to various men over many different generations.

The biblical account tells of men who saw and spoke to a supernatural entity that promised certain events would transpire, and
they shared this knowledge with others. After these prophecies
had been fulfilled, all were convinced they had been contacted by
God. Even those that followed other gods were said to change
their beliefs after seeing extraordinary events unfold. Indeed, it
is difficult to conceive of another reason for countless people to
convert to monotheistic belief in the God of Abraham, given the
number of competing ideas to choose from.

A growing wealth of archaeological finds aligns well with the
Old Testament. Uncovered inscriptions and records have allowed
researchers to glean more information about ancient cultures,
practices, customs, leaders, names, geography, events, and so

on—data that validates the biblical account in ways that could not have been anticipated. Artifacts such as the Mesha Stele and the Tel Dan Stele establish the existence of the ancient Israelites, their God named Yahweh, the reign of King David, and other historical facts some scholars once thought to be errors or even outright fabrications by Bible authors.

If the basic biblical outline of history is true, these are exactly the types of findings one would expect.

CRITICISM OF THE BIBLE

While it is unquestionably an exceptional literary work, not all are convinced of the Bible's veracity. Let's look at some common challenges leveled against it.

"THE BIBLE DESCRIBES IMPOSSIBLE EVENTS."

A concern for many is that the Bible depicts things that defy the laws of nature. The Old Testament alone contains a wealth of stories in which Abraham, Noah, Moses, and many other people witnessed miraculous or supernatural events.

We know that certain limitations exist within our universe. There is no way to defy these laws of nature apart from supernatural power. For this reason, if you saw someone summon a column of fire down from the sky, or ascend into the clouds, you would probably listen to them very carefully.

A creator attempting to introduce himself, prove his power, or convey an important message to us would certainly do best to accompany his message with such feats. If he were unable to bend the very laws of nature he claims to control, how could he expect to convince anyone? If the biblical narrative didn't mention any miracles, detractors would seize on this immediately—and rightfully so. If it were really God, he would *prove* it.

The only objection left is simply "Miracles are impossible. Everyone knows miracles violate the laws of nature." This is true—which is why they provide such compelling proof for the observer. Miracles usually cause witnesses to believe something completely and instantly.

If you watched a spectacular event unfold that violated laws of nature, you'd probably tell everyone you know. This appears to be exactly what the Bible's authors recorded. If the biblical account is any indication, these individuals were convinced that Abraham's God existed, made himself known to them, predicted the future, and performed miracles. Finding this many people to falsely claim they witnessed such things is very unlikely.

The events described in the Bible were usually witnessed by many people, and were not limited to only one person's account; the effects were obvious to outside observers. Additionally, the revelations identifying God and his purpose were consistently coupled with a supernatural miracle or promise to confirm their authenticity—not once to one person, but throughout time, to provide proof to many different witnesses.

If the God of the Bible *couldn't* perform supernatural miracles, there would be no reason to entertain the possibility that it's true.

"THE BIBLE SAYS EVERYTHING WAS CREATED IN SIX DAYS."

Sort of. Maybe not at all. The Bible often uses dramatic Eastern imagery to simplify a concept where, as here, the mystery behind it is yet unknown to man.

Why insist on interpreting this beautiful illustration literally? Does the validity of the entire message truly hinge on whether the "days" were literal *24-hour days* from the perspective of the earth? Can a day even be measured prior to the existence of the sun and earth? Some believe each day represents a far longer time span, just as a "week" clearly refers to seven years in other passages. Each day of creation could conceivably represent millions of years. Perhaps, at their inception, the laws of nature initially allowed time to move exponentially faster. Anything is possible. It seems petty, if not unwise, to dogmatically assert that the universe was created in 144 hours. We simply cannot know.

What if a great deal of time passed between the initial creation of the universe, and the six-day preparation described in the first chapter of Genesis? Some Christians haven't even considered the possibility that the earth existed for billions of years before it was prepared for mankind. But read the first two verses of the Bible:

> In the beginning of God's preparing the heavens and the earth—the earth hath existed waste and void, and dark-ness [is] on the face of the deep, and the Spirit of God fluttering on the face of the waters. (Genesis 1:1–2 YLT)

This plainly suggests that the universe already existed and the earth was covered in water *before* the six-day account even began. As for how long, who knows? Such an interpretation is certainly reasonable, particularly in light of the original Hebrew.

Objections to a literal six-day creation are most often raised by opponents of theism, who endorse macroevolution as a favored explanation for the origin of life. As we've already seen, that idea fails miserably: it starts in the middle, and merely passes the problem back up to another area of research. Nonetheless, its proponents assert that the creation account is pure conjecture and lacks falsifiability. In other words, they say there is no way to disprove it scientifically. This is true. Meanwhile, the fossil record provides irrefutable evidence of explosions in plant and animal species at various points in history—things evolutionary hypotheses can never explain, but a creator certainly does.

The only evolution we see is confined to each type of organism. How many generations of apple seeds must we plant in order to prove it can never yield a peach? In reality, nothing could be found to refute evolutionary theory any more soundly than what has already been discovered. As our knowledge grows, it has become increasingly clear that the very science that supposedly refutes creationism is in fact its key witness.

However science may choose to explain it, the Bible plainly states that God created man and woman at some point in the past.[6] Science will continue to change its hypotheses as new information is uncovered, yet the colorful writing style of the Bible has survived millennium after millennium in its elegant simplicity, unable to be refuted.

Scholars understand that stories and analogies found in works of ancient literature must be evaluated within the context of their original culture and language. But many people read and interpret the Bible in a very strict literal sense, leading them to reach strange conclusions—or reject it entirely.

To be sure, the Bible does not hold itself out as a science textbook. It was not intended to teach biology or physics. Nor is it a timeline designed to calculate the precise age of the universe. Critiquing it as though it were simply misses the greater point, which is to ask: *Can we rely on its basic premise?*

"THE BIBLE SAYS THE EARTH IS FLAT."

The Bible contains phrases that illustrate the extents of the world, such as "the four corners of the earth" in Isaiah 11:12. It has been suggested that the author believed the earth was flat, and that this proves the Bible is false and inconsistent with modern science. However, this phrase is often used to represent the four cardinal directions. Tellingly, the same book later mentions "the circle of the earth."[7] Clearly, these two descriptive phrases are not the writer's focus: they are used in passing, and were never intended to reveal the shape of our planet.

Scientists long thought the universe was in an eternal or static state, but they were wrong: we now know the universe is expanding outward from a central point of origin. Isaiah 40:22, written thousands of years ago, states that God "stretcheth out the heavens as a curtain, and spreadeth them out as a tent to dwell in"—a description strikingly consistent with modern physical cosmology. And in what is thought to be the oldest book of the Bible, Job 26:7 states that God "hangs the Earth on nothing," which aptly describes a planet floating in the void of space. At the time it was written, this information could only have been known by the creator of the universe. Was the Bible thousands of years ahead of science? It is certainly possible.

In any case, some descriptions are not to be taken literally. Do modern writers really believe our sun "rises" and "sets"? Of course not. People using these phrases aren't ignorant of the earth's rotation; it is merely descriptive. The use of such language today could lead future readers to think we did not understand Earth's rotation—but they'd be wrong. Would they discredit an entire work based on their misunderstanding? Let's hope not.

"THE BIBLE ISN'T THE FIRST TO MENTION A FLOOD."

It has been suggested that the Bible is merely a compilation of religious folklore that preceded it. Many point to ancient pagan myths and other literary works to suggest that Christianity was plagiarized. For example, the Deluge Tablet predates any written records discovered for the Bible, and it contains an inscription of the *Epic of Gilgamesh*—a story with remarkably close parallels to the biblical account of Adam and Eve and the great flood of Noah.

The Sumerian King List is an ancient list of Mesopotamian rulers and the lengths of their reigns in the region of modern-day Iraq. Various copies have been unearthed, with the oldest dating back to approximately 2000 BC. Interestingly, it is divided into two parts: those who ruled before a massive flood (antediluvian), and those since. One of the kings listed, Enmebaragesi, has been verified by archaeological findings, and his name is also mentioned in the *Epic of Gilgamesh*.

Startlingly similar descriptions of the world's creation and a subsequent deluge to eradicate evil are also recorded in the Atra-Hasis tablets, the Eridu Genesis tablet, and writings by Berossus.

There are hundreds of similar accounts across various cultures and languages, usually describing a man who constructed a large boat to help his family escape a flood that once engulfed the earth.

Skeptics have asserted that these other ancient artifacts really originated the concept of a man created in a garden, the introduction of evil into the world, and a great flood—and that the Bible simply copied them. But if all of these things really *did* happen, wouldn't they find their way into many other oral traditions and literary works?

If large-scale flooding really occurred, wouldn't it be odd if the Bible contained the only record of it? Doesn't it make sense that other sources would also mention the same pivotal moments in human history? If many literary works echo the same elements and substantiate one another, it is logical to conclude that these stories were recorded because they actually happened.

This is precisely the result any historian would expect if these events took place. It would be absurd to dismiss an account as false simply because it is corroborated by other ancient works.

"THE BIBLE CONTAINS ERRORS."

If it is written in English, then yes—it certainly does. We know this because every English translation contains differences that contradict other versions. Compare any two; they will differ from each other, often significantly.

It is critical to remember that our *translations* are not equivalent to the original, and will always contain deviations. The Bible was not written in English, and our modern translations are far removed from the original languages. Some even drew from Latin versions, suffering from additional layers of confusion. It would be a grave mistake to regard any English translation as inerrant. Most contain numerous contradictions and errors that are easy to spot (as we will see later) and make it difficult to discern the true intent of the original message.

Our oldest manuscripts of the Bible have sustained few, if any, transmission errors. They are essentially identical to the originals. So the original text is valid—but what about our interpretation of it? When questions arise as to the correct meaning of a passage, the Hebrew and Greek texts should be consulted. And now, with the help of a concordance or online study tools, anyone can easily look up the precise meaning of an original Hebrew or Greek word to glean more insight into the true message recorded in these ancient writings.

CONCLUSION

The Bible is the most unique literary work of all time. No other text, religious or otherwise, even comes close. If our creator left a message for humanity, it is the only viable option.

The Bible's authors describe an intimately involved deity who made promises to his created beings, interacted with them, told them their future, and gave them guidance on how to live. But how can we determine whether the message is true?

CHAPTER 6

CONTACT

Three things cannot be long hidden:
the sun, the moon, and the truth.

— BUDDHA

I F THE BIBLE was divinely inspired, God would remove all doubt and provide us with irrefutable proof, right? Surely mankind would know if a supernatural deity contacted us. There would be stories. Writings. Witnesses. The word would spread very quickly, and could not be contained as eyewitnesses shared their accounts with one another.

If people saw proof of God's existence with their own eyes, it would change lives. Redefine priorities. Disrupt the system. The world would mark such a momentous event on every calendar.

The Gregorian calendar is the international standard used worldwide. But why? What historic event took place over 2,000 years ago? What was significant enough to define "year zero"? Surely humanity did not come to agree on just any random date to be the reference point for all time.

History points to the existence of a man named Jesus of Nazareth. So who was he, a great magician? A smart teacher?

Ghandi was a wise teacher too, but we did not reset the calendar to honor him.

We are told that Jesus paid particular attention to the common people, and he was criticized for befriending and associating with less-respected members of society. But is this enough to justify setting the reference point for all recorded history? No. Mother Teresa ministered to plenty of less fortunate people herself.

Some say Jesus performed many miracles: healing the sick, walking on water, restoring sight to the blind, feeding a large crowd, turning water into wine, raising a man named Lazarus from the dead, and so on. Yes, assertions like these would have to precede such a momentous change. Regardless of whether these miracles actually took place, it is clear that extremely bold claims must have been made to warrant resetting the year count.

Whatever happened two thousand years ago is not merely a part of the historical record: it is the primary reference point from which we date all other events. This is beyond question, otherwise the world would put a different year number on its documents.

The label BC stands for *Before Christ*, and AD is an abbreviation for *Anno Domini*, which is Latin for "In the year of the Lord." (Note that contrary to popular thought, AD does not mean "after death.") They identify the years before and after the approximate birth of Jesus of Nazareth.[1] In an effort to abandon the overtly religious meaning of these labels, many modern writings have adopted BCE and CE, which represent *Before Current Era* and *Current Era*. Still, the year numbers remain unchanged.

Many wonderful teachers, prophets, leaders, bright minds, and good people left a proud legacy behind. But the year was not set to zero for Confucius, Buddha, Muhammad, Newton, or Einstein. This pivotal role in history belongs to one man: Jesus.

His followers believed he performed miracles while healing and caring for people. But many others have represented themselves as having supernatural gifts before, and that wasn't enough to get the world's attention. So what made Jesus stand out? One key difference is that very few people throughout history have ever claimed to be a deity. Some said they were prophets, which is much harder to disprove, but Jesus said he was a god—*the* God.

The gravity of this assertion is really quite breathtaking. You may even think it sounds a little... insane.

A BOLD CLAIM

The Jewish people in Jesus' time were intimately familiar with the Tanakh (the Old Testament), which foretold a great leader would come to unite the tribes of Israel. The word *messiah* in Hebrew (and *Christos* in Greek) refers to a future ruler anointed by God.

The Israelites were expecting this messiah to arrive on the scene at any moment. They believed he would be a great and powerful leader from the lineage of King David who would rise to power, usher in an age of peace on Earth, and reign over all nations forever.[2]

Jesus, however, didn't just claim to be the king of the Jews: he claimed to be *God*. This was frowned upon by Jewish leaders, to put it mildly. They saw it as outright blasphemy—an offense for which Jewish law prescribed death by stoning. As a Jew himself, Jesus was subject to their laws, and many of them were looking for an opportunity to swiftly end his life. Here's how the Bible describes one particular run-in between Jesus and the Jews:

> The Jews who were there gathered around him, saying, "How long will you keep us in suspense? If you are the Messiah, tell us plainly."
>
> Jesus answered, "I did tell you, but you do not believe. ... I and the Father are one."
>
> Again his Jewish opponents picked up stones to stone him, but Jesus said to them, "I have shown you many good works from the Father. For which of these do you stone me?"

"We are not stoning you for any good work," they replied, "but for blasphemy, because you, a mere man, claim to be God." (John 10:24–25,30–33 NIV)

Two things are clear. First, the Jews definitely understood Jesus' claim of divinity. Second, they flatly rejected it. In their view, the messiah's arrival would be obvious: a leader endowed with immense political power, great wealth, and royal lineage. The Jewish high priests paid particular attention to appearances, especially how they dressed and the company they kept. Jesus was a peasant surrounded by people of lesser status. He was not the neatly polished leader they were anticipating.

Jesus had to know his assertion would ultimately cost him his life. Eventually he was arrested and delivered to the authorities to be tried. However, he maintained his claim during the trial, even as he faced the penalty of death:

But Jesus remained silent and gave no answer. Again the high priest asked him, "Are you the Messiah, the Son of the Blessed One?"

"I AM," said Jesus. "And you will see the Son of Man sitting at the right hand of the Mighty One and coming on the clouds of heaven."

The high priest tore his clothes. "Why do we need any more witnesses?" he asked. "You have heard the blasphemy. What do you think?" They all condemned him as worthy of death. (Mark 14:61–64 NIV)

The Jewish priests were shocked and appalled when Jesus identified himself as "I AM." As noted before, this was the name of God revealed to Moses, and Jesus' use of it was not well-received, as he was clearly claiming to be equal to God. He also spoke of seeing their ancestor Abraham, who had long been dead, and said he existed before him:

"You are not yet fifty years old," they said to him, "and you have seen Abraham!"

"Very truly I tell you," Jesus answered, "before Abraham was born, I AM!" (John 8:57–58 NIV)

Since only God could have been alive that long ago, this was again a claim of divinity. But to prevent any misunderstanding, Jesus again identified himself by the name of God. They were eager to kill him on the spot—something they would soon succeed at.

The Bible describes Jesus commanding others to honor him as God (John 5:23–24), accepting their worship (Matthew 8:2; John 9:35–39), and letting them refer to him as their Lord (Matthew 14:33; 8:8) and the Christ (Matthew 16:16). He made many more claims of divinity than these examples.[3] There is no question that Jesus was going around claiming to be God: his life ended abruptly as a result.

Jesus' assertion that he is God is either true or false. Either he was simply stating what he believed to be true, or he was a very twisted individual. This claim leaves only three possibilities:

1. Jesus was insane

2. Jesus was a liar

3. Jesus is God

If his claim was false, then Jesus was either a lunatic making an honest mistake, or an evil deceiver bent on misleading people. But if his claim is true, then Jesus is God, just as he said. We can try to dodge the question or explain it away, but in the end, these are the only three options we are left with—so let's consider each.

Could a *lunatic* speak with such poise and authority? Could he demonstrate concern and compassion for others, and form coherent, consistent, and wise messages still heralded today as the key to abundant life? This is neither likely nor logical.

Why would a *liar* who is engaged in a grand deception teach his followers to always tell the truth? Why would a scam artist command others to help the needy instead of hoarding wealth for himself? Above all, no one would let his own life be taken for a claim he knows is a lie. This explanation makes no sense either.

Aside from being implausible, these two possibilities are also extraordinarily unlikely to result in a global impact of the magnitude required to reset the calendar to the time of his birth—a fact that cannot be ignored. An ego trip is not enough to gain such a momentous following. The earth has been home to many con men and quacks whose names we may never hear, but Jesus is known the world over.

Jesus is considered by virtually every non-Christian religion to be a good man or a wise teacher. However, he ruled both of these out when he claimed to be God.[4] We are welcome to reject his claim, but if we do, we must concede that Jesus was either evil or crazy to have said such a thing—certainly not good or wise.

Ultimately, we must either accept or reject Jesus' assertion. But before we do, let us examine the historical record found in other writings, so that our decision is not based solely on the Bible.

THE HISTORY

It is well-established that Jesus of Nazareth walked the earth over 2,000 years ago claiming to be God. He only lived to be about thirty-three years old—a short lifetime in which to gain perpetual worldwide notoriety.

Remarkably, Jesus only began his ministry after age thirty. This means most everything we know about him stems from a brief period spanning about three years, during which he remained within just a few hundred miles of his birthplace in Bethlehem. He did not spend his life jetting around the globe making appearances and giving interviews to promote a movement. He did not have a prestigious position, great wealth, or modern global communication to aid him. Yet the reach of his life is limitless even now, more than two thousand years later.

Jesus' life had a profound impact that reverberates to this day, even among non-Christians. One of the earliest known references to substantiate this comes from a first-century historian named Flavius Josephus in his *Jewish Antiquities*. As a Jew, Josephus was no doubt critical of Jesus—yet he openly acknowledges that Jesus was referred to as "Christ":

> [H]e assembled the sanhedrin of judges, and brought before them the brother of Jesus, who was called Christ, whose name was James, and some others; and when he had formed an accusation against them as breakers of the law, he delivered them to be stoned...[5]

He also documents the imprisonment and subsequent execution of John the Baptist, a biblical figure who had baptized many people and was gaining a great following that made Herod uneasy.[6] Written by a critic rather than a Christian sympathizer, these records clearly demonstrate that a man named Jesus was referred to as the Christ; he had a brother named James; his associates were gaining popularity that threatened political leadership; and his followers were being severely punished.[7]

Tacitus has been called the greatest historian of ancient Rome. The *Annals*, mentioned previously, is a well-respected historical account that has been referred to as his crowning achievement. About eighty years after Christ's execution, Tacitus—also not a fan of Jesus—recorded how Nero blamed the Christians for the fires in Rome:

> Nero fastened the guilt and inflicted the most exquisite tortures on a class hated for their abominations, called Christians by the populace. Christus, from whom the name had its origin, suffered the extreme penalty during the reign of Tiberius at the hands of one of our procurators, Pontius Pilatus, and a most mischievous superstition, thus checked for the moment, again broke out not only in Judæa, the first source of the evil, but even in Rome...

Accordingly, an arrest was first made of all who pleaded guilty; then, upon their information, an immense multitude was convicted, not so much of the crime of firing the city, as of hatred against mankind. Mockery of every sort was added to their deaths. Covered with the skins of beasts, they were torn by dogs and perished, or were nailed to crosses, or were doomed to the flames and burnt, to serve as a nightly illumination, when daylight had expired.[8]

These records establish many important details about "Christus," the leader of the Christians.[9] They tell us Jesus was put to death by Pontius Pilate, and that a "most mischievous superstition" about him originated from Judea. They do not reveal exactly what the belief was, but it clearly prompted strong devotion from Jesus' followers, despite the threat of torment and certain death: they were being tortured, fed to dogs, nailed to crosses, and set ablaze for their loyalty to Christ.

By this time, Christians were being convicted and punished in droves—not for specific crimes, but for their beliefs. Pliny the Younger was a Roman imperial magistrate who began serving under emperor Trajan around AD 100, about seventy years after Christ's crucifixion. One of the challenges he faced was how to deal with the growing number of Jesus' followers. In what may be one of the longest letters addressing emperor Trajan—indicative of its importance—Pliny describes the trial and punishment of many suspected believers:

I interrogated them whether they were Christians; if they confessed, I repeated the question twice, adding threats at the same time; and if they still persevered, I ordered them to be immediately punished. ...

They affirmed the whole of their guilt, or their error, was, that they met on a certain stated day before it was light, and addressed themselves in a form of prayer to Christ, as to some god, binding themselves by a solemn oath, not for the purposes of any wicked design, but never to commit any fraud, theft, or adultery; never to falsify their word, nor deny a trust when they should be called upon to deliver it up; after which, it was their custom to separate, and then reassemble, to eat in common a harmless meal.[10]

Pliny was responsible for torturing and killing many Christians. Yet in his personal correspondence he freely admits that, as best he can tell, there is no crime being committed; Jesus' followers are merely taking an oath not to lie, cheat, or steal, sharing a meal together, and praying to Christ as if he were deity:

> In consequence of this their declaration, I judged it the more necessary to endeavour to extort the real truth, by putting two female slaves to the torture, who were said to officiate in their religious functions; but all I could discover was, that these people were actuated by an absurd and excessive superstition. ...
>
> For, it appears to be a matter highly deserving your consideration; more especially as great numbers must be involved in the danger of these prosecutions, which have already extended, and are still likely to extend, to persons of all ranks and ages, and even of both sexes. In fact, this contagious superstition is not confined to the cities only, but has spread its infection among the neighbouring villages and country. Nevertheless, it still seems possible to restrain its progress.[11]

With only this historical record in view, it is clear his followers believed Jesus was a deity—a conviction they were willing to die for because of a "contagious superstition." We aren't told what convinced them, but his followers were growing very rapidly.

Sometime around AD 165–180, Lucian of Samosata wrote *The Death of Peregrine*, a satirical story that offers a description of how early Christians believed and behaved:

> The Christians, you know, worship a man to this day—the distinguished personage who introduced their

novel rites, and was crucified on that account. ... The activity of these people, in dealing with any matter that affects their community, is something extraordinary; they spare no trouble, no expense. ...

You see, these misguided creatures start with the general conviction that they are immortal for all time, which explains the contempt of death and voluntary self-devotion which are so common among them; and then it was impressed on them by their original lawgiver that they are all brothers, from the moment that they are converted, and deny the gods of Greece, and worship the crucified sage, and live after his laws. All this they take quite on trust, with the result that they despise all worldly goods alike, regarding them merely as common property.[12]

Though unflattering, this passage records the basic premise of the Christian faith less than 150 years after Jesus' crucifixion: They worship a leader who started their cause and was crucified for it. They look after one another, regard each other as brothers and sisters, give little value to worldly goods, reject polytheism, and believe they will live forever.

Finally, we will consider an ancient debate that took place in writing. Sextus Julius Africanus was a Christian that lived about a century and a half after Jesus' death. He completed a five-book history of the world, the *Chronografiai*, sometime around AD 220. In it, he challenged and responded to other works by non-Christian writers that mentioned strange events occurring at the hour of Christ's crucifixion, including a great earthquake and darkness that fell over the earth for hours. These phenomena are described in the biblical account of Christ's execution, and were believed by Christians like Africanus to be supernatural confirmation of Christ's divinity at his death. However, non-Christians (such as Thallus and Phlegon) sought to dispel this notion with natural explanations for these events, such as by attributing the darkness to a solar eclipse. Africanus dismisses their conclusions as impossible given the position of the sun during the time of Passover, which is when Christ's crucifixion occurred.[13]

Of course, these writings don't prove that the darkness or the earthquake were supernatural signs, or that Jesus was God. But it proves conclusively that both Christians and non-Christians were in agreement on the fact that some very strange events took place when Jesus was executed—things that demanded explanation.

Given these and many other corroborating written records, the biblical account of these events seems extraordinarily reliable.

DIGGING UP THE PAST

Our insight into history isn't limited only to literature. Many archaeological discoveries have been uncovered in recent years that shed light on the history of Jesus. In 1961, a block called the Pilate Stone was found in Caesarea Maritima during the excavation of an ancient theater. This block contains the only inscription known to identify Pontius Pilate. Before this discovery, some rejected the accuracy of the biblical account, which identifies him as the Roman official responsible for Jesus' execution:

> As soon as the chief priests and their officials saw him, they shouted, "Crucify! Crucify!" But Pilate answered, "You take him and crucify him. As for me, I find no basis for a charge against him." The Jews insisted, "We have a law, and according to that law he must die, because he claimed to be the Son of God."
>
> When Pilate heard this, he was even more afraid, and he went back inside the palace. "Where do you come from?" he asked Jesus, but Jesus gave him no answer. "Do you refuse to speak to me?" Pilate said. "Don't you realize I have power either to free you or to crucify you?"[14]

Critics suggested Pontius Pilate was simply a fabrication by Bible authors prior to this important find. Today, of course, all scholars agree that he existed. The Bible has proven remarkably accurate on details that some historians previously rejected or could not confirm, but have now been authenticated by new discoveries.

Pilate wasn't bluffing. Just days after Jesus rode into Jerusalem on a donkey and was greeted by a great multitude of worshipers, Pilate reluctantly delivered him up for crucifixion. He tried to appease them by offering other solutions, but the Jewish chief priests wanted Jesus executed for calling himself their king, which they said defied Caesar's authority. It is for this reason they sought to have the sentence carried out by the Romans.

Pilate placed a sign bearing the inscription "Jesus of Nazareth, the King of the Jews" at the top of the cross, despite protests from the Jewish leaders.[15] During his crucifixion, witnesses taunted him, saying that if he were truly the messiah he should just come down from the cross and save himself.[16] As his bones slipped out of joint, the soldiers crucifying him offered Jesus vinegar to drink. Then they divided his garments among themselves and cast lots for his clothing (similar to rolling dice), all while he hung nailed to the cross before them—thirsting, suffering, dying.

Regardless of one's religious beliefs, the story of Jesus' life, works, and crucifixion is certainly riveting. The first four books of the New Testament that contain this account are called the *gospels*. "Gospel" is an Old English word adapted from the Greek term *euangelion*, which means "good news" or "good message." When people *evangelize*, they are said to be spreading the good news about Jesus found in these books.

But wait... What good news?

The history of Jesus is absolutely tragic: People met a man whom they believed to be the God of Abraham. They followed him. They loved him. They believed he was the long-awaited messiah. But then he was suddenly put to death.

That doesn't seem like good news at all.

CHAPTER 7

MYSTERY

The supreme function of reason is to show man
that some things are beyond reason.

— BLAISE PASCAL

A NYONE can claim to be a prophet. They could even claim to be God. A cult leader may be able to convince others he has the power to perform miracles. But when a false messiah dies, the movement dies with him—and soon his following disappears.

We've seen it before. Jim Jones, David Koresh, Sun Myung Moon, Charles Manson, and many others have claimed to be the messiah, the Christ, or a deity. After their death, however, the movement fizzled out. Their own mortality proved they were not what they claimed to be.

The messiah the Jews anticipated was supposed to become a great ruler, not get executed on a cross. During his travels, the crowds around Jesus confirmed their understanding of this when they stated, "We have heard from the law that the Christ will remain forever."[1] If Jesus were really the Christ, they expected him to stick around. So once he was betrayed for thirty pieces of silver by Judas Iscariot, taken into custody, subjected to a hasty trial, and then put to death by crucifixion, the movement should have ended. But this time was different.

It certainly seemed like it was all over. Jesus' followers were devastated. The unflattering biblical account says his friends did not rush to his defense, but instead hid like cowards. Once Jesus was taken into custody, his disciple Peter denied knowing him three separate times.[2] After watching the humiliating defeat of the one they called Lord, Christ's eleven closest followers scattered in fear.[3] In their absence, a wealthy stranger named Joseph asked Pilate for his body after Jesus was pronounced dead by Roman soldiers. This man provided a proper resting place—an empty tomb that belonged to his family—while Christ's dearest friends were nowhere to be found.

It seems Christianity should have died, along with Jesus of Nazareth, on that dark and devastating afternoon. If a modern cult leader were executed by the authorities, would his followers sacrifice their own lives to continue spreading his brand of religion? Not likely. Even Jesus' most devoted followers denied they knew him hours after he was taken into custody—well before his trial and execution.

But recall the ancient historians' descriptions of Christians who were being burned alive, fed to dogs, crucified, tortured, and killed for their faith after Jesus' death. What made his followers turn from cowardly to courageous? For some reason, they were suddenly galvanized with unwavering loyalty, and willing to spread the message at any cost—even in the face of these unimaginable, horrific threats. Something huge turned this movement around, and it went from nearly dead to resetting the world calendar.

So, what happened *after* Jesus was killed? This brings us to another fundamental difference between Jesus and other religious figures: the resurrection. Christians believe Jesus rose from the dead three days after his crucifixion and then met with many people, as described in the Book of Acts:

> We are witnesses of everything he did in the country of
> the Jews and in Jerusalem. They killed him by hanging
> him on a cross, but God raised him from the dead on the
> third day and caused him to be seen. He was not seen by
> all the people, but by witnesses whom God had already
> chosen—by us who ate and drank with him after he rose
> from the dead. (Acts 10:39–41 NIV)

Early believers were clear that Christ's resurrection was a real
physical event, and that hundreds of people witnessed his return
to life over a period of forty days. These people believed they
met, spoke to, and ate and drank with Jesus after he rose from the
dead in a new physical body—not merely a ghost, a vision, or an
apparition, but a real live person.

Curiously, Christ's *teachings* aren't emphasized nearly as often
as his *resurrection*. This is because the resurrection is the cornerstone of belief in Jesus as God. As Paul wrote in his letter to the
Corinthians, "And if Christ has not been raised, our preaching is
useless and so is your faith."[4] In other words, if Jesus hadn't really
died on the cross and rose to life again, there would be nothing
for them to place their trust in. While there have been many great
teachers and philosophers, none had power over death; only God
has that. In rising to life, Jesus proved his identity.

Letters and writings outside the Bible confirm that Jesus' bodily
resurrection was central to the Christian faith. Ignatius, an early
believer in Christ, wrote a letter to the Trallians just before he was
killed in Rome which mentions

> Jesus Christ, who was of the race of David, of the Virgin
> Mary: who was truly born, and did eat and drink, was
> truly persecuted under Pontius Pilate, was truly crucified,
> and died, in the sight of those in heaven, and of those on
> earth, and of those under the earth. Who also was truly
> raised from the dead, by his Father; after the same manner
> as he will also raise up us who believe in him, by Christ
> Jesus, without whom we have no true life.[5]

This is the same belief for which Ignatius was later martyred. Many historical references to belief in Jesus' physical resurrection were recorded by other ancient writers, including Clement of Rome, Polycarp, Justin Martyr and Tertullian.[6]

If Christ came back to life, consider what it would have been like from the perspective of the eyewitnesses. Many of them were present at his crucifixion—but then personally saw, spoke with, or even touched Jesus in real life days after mourning his death. For them, this would be irrefutable proof that he was God. Jesus promised he would give them life. And now, having witnessed firsthand his power over death, it was clear that he could deliver on that promise. They took this belief to their grave, and many endured unbearable torture and painful execution as a result.

But if Jesus didn't really rise from the dead, then what took place? It's difficult to imagine an alternative event that would lead to the same outcome. Non-Christian historians recorded that Jesus' followers believed in a "contagious superstition," and that "a most mischievous superstition, thus checked for the moment, again broke out not only in Judæa, the first source of the evil, but even in Rome." Why would executing Jesus of Nazareth keep this superstition in check only for the moment? Killing their leader should have stopped it at once. It shouldn't have broken out again, and certainly not even faster than before.

There is no logical reason for these events to have occurred unless Jesus actually came back to life. The resurrection is the most viable explanation for everything history attests to.

WHAT REALLY HAPPENED?

The historical record is clear: Jesus was a real person who lived in the first century. He was a Jewish teacher from Galilee that was crucified under the authority of Pontius Pilate. He was worshiped as God by his followers, and was put to death for his claims. His body went missing shortly after his death. Afterward, belief in his divinity exploded virally for some reason, prompting leaders of the day to attempt to contain the spread of its influence. The facts point unavoidably to a miraculous event. We can either accept Christ's resurrection as true, or reject it as a fraud. But wait, could all of this be the result of an elaborate hoax?

Let us objectively consider the evidence for and against the claim that Jesus rose from the dead by evaluating the biblical account of the resurrection.

FALSE WITNESSES

It would have been extremely difficult to recruit people to lie about Christ's resurrection. This would have been a slap in the face to Jesus, who directed them to always tell the truth, as well as a violation of the Ten Commandments set forth in the Bible.

But there is another very strong reason to believe that Jesus' followers were being honest. In his letter to the Corinthians, Paul openly identifies individuals and groups of witnesses in Jerusalem:

> [T]hat he was buried, that he was raised on the third day according to the Scriptures, and that he appeared to Cephas, and then to the Twelve.
>
> After that, he appeared to more than five hundred of the brothers and sisters at the same time, most of whom are still living, though some have fallen asleep.
>
> Then he appeared to James, then to all the apostles...[7]

Providing a witness list wasn't necessary to try to deceive people, and doing so would only invite others to challenge their account of these events. More importantly, perpetrators of a hoax would not identify themselves and place their lives in danger to promote a lie. Followers of Jesus had just witnessed his execution, and knew that they, too, might be hunted down and killed soon. They would not have revealed their identities unless they *truly* believed what they were attesting to.

Obviously none of these witnesses would be willing to endure torture or martyrdom just to keep a hoax going. When pressed, they would have denied it immediately if it were a fraud. But history assures us they did not: countless Christians were being ruthlessly slaughtered simply for their beliefs.

REPUTABLE WITNESSES

It would be best to choose reputable witnesses to bolster a fraudulent claim. The Jewish culture at that time regarded the testimony of women as virtually worthless. If Jesus' resurrection was faked, why choose to make women the first witnesses?[8]

Any astute conspirator would have selected male witnesses to give their story more credibility, yet the biblical authors made no such effort. It seems they were simply giving an accurate account of what took place, no matter the cost.

FRIENDLY WITNESSES

If you were telling a lie, you wouldn't want to list your enemies as witnesses. Yet the biblical account includes an admission from a Roman soldier responsible for crucifying Christ. After Jesus cried out from the cross "It is finished" and exhaled his final breath, we are told that the soldier standing before him exclaimed, "Truly this man was the Son of God."[9] Had it been false, this reckless fabrication would be all too easy for others to disprove: they could simply ask the soldier—or anyone else present that day.

Similarly, the biblical account states that the Roman soldiers assigned to protect Christ's body witnessed a miracle as the great stone sealing his tomb was rolled away by an angel. If this were a lie, it would be best to list co-conspirators as witnesses—people in on the hoax, rather than Jesus' enemies. Instead, they were encouraged to ask the soldiers themselves. Adding details such as these would undermine their claims—unless, of course, these events had actually transpired and were easy for anyone to verify.

THE MISSING BODY

It is impossible to stage a resurrection hoax without first stealing the corpse. So how did it get removed from the tomb?

Jesus' death was verified by the Roman soldiers, who pierced his side with a spear as he hung from the cross, and watched blood and water pour forth from the wound.[10] Pilate then allowed his body to be prepared for burial. Shortly after it was placed in the tomb, the Jews came to Pilate and requested that he assign guards to watch after it. They suspected that Jesus taught he would rise from the dead, and they didn't want anyone to steal his body to further such rumors. So Pilate verified the body was inside the tomb, secured the stone that blocked it with a seal to ensure it was not disturbed, and stationed a group of soldiers to keep watch.[11] Unfortunately for the high priests, these extreme measures had the unintended consequence of proving that the body could not possibly have been stolen.

The biblical account says the soldiers assigned to guard the tomb saw an angel descend from heaven and roll away the stone in front, exposing that it was empty. At this, the guards trembled with fear and left to report what they had seen to the high priests, rather than their Roman superiors. The priests gave the soldiers large sums of money and instructed them to say that Christ's disciples came by night, and stole him away while the guards slept. Because the penalty for a soldier to fall asleep or abandon his post was death, the priests assured the soldiers safety should their story get back around to the governor.[12]

The excuse concocted by the priests is essentially the same hoax argument leveled against the resurrection today. However, that version of events is riddled with significant problems:

- Roman soldiers would not be willing to risk execution just to take a nap—certainly not all at the same time. These ruthless centurions, who were responsible for crucifying lawbreakers, were well aware of the severe consequences awaiting those who abdicated their duties.

- Thieves couldn't have rolled the giant stone away silently while the guards slept—it took multiple men to move it into place. The noise of grinding rock would have awakened any that dared to sleep.

- Had the guards really been asleep, they wouldn't know who took the body. And if they had truly seen the thieves, why did they let them escape? A group of men hauling a heavy corpse would be no match for a conditioned Roman soldier.

- None of Jesus' followers were ever captured or punished for stealing his body. If the soldiers' story was true, why wasn't anyone prosecuted?

- Thieves would not have bothered to leave the burial cloths behind. It would take far too long to unwrap the body. Thieves would have simply grabbed it and ran.

- All of his followers were still hiding in fear, denying that they knew Jesus. There is no logical explanation for their sudden willingness to stand up for him, risk death, take on a group of Roman soldiers, move a massive stone, and steal a corpse... all for a lie.

Some have suggested Christ's body was never there to begin with. However, there can be no question that the body was present when Pilate posted the soldiers in front of the tomb, because the entire purpose of sealing and securing it was to ensure that the remains would not be disturbed or removed. The guards themselves certainly would have confirmed that the very body they were charged with protecting—on penalty of *death*—was there before the entrance was sealed. If it were missing, they would be the first to report it, so as to avoid being executed.

If Jesus' body were anywhere to be found, his enemies would have produced it immediately in order to put an end to the rumors of his resurrection. No one ever located Christ's corpse.

EXTRAORDINARY CLAIMS

Finally, if this were false, why allege Jesus was around for forty days, and was seen by multitudes of witnesses? This could easily be disproved by anyone in Jerusalem. It would be much harder to refute the claim that Jesus appeared before one or two people.

If it was just a scam, why bother claiming Jesus was *physically* resurrected? Why not say that his resurrection was to a spiritual form, which left his old body intact in the tomb? Or why not base the faith on philosophical teachings, instead of historical events? No one could argue with these claims, and they would be much easier to defend—yet the eyewitness accounts go much further.

Some of Jesus' closest followers did not believe reports of his resurrection until they witnessed it themselves. One skeptic believed only after touching the scars on Jesus' hands, and placing his fingers inside the hole where the spear had pierced his side.[13] Jesus then criticized their unbelief. These are certainly not the strongest statements the authors of a hoax could make. On the other hand, they are precisely the reactions one would expect.

Early Christians didn't sacrifice their lives just to defend some teachings. They believed Jesus was God, and that he had died, risen to life, visited them, and returned to heaven. This is the only rational reason they would be willing to die as martyrs. It also explains why the spread of Christianity couldn't be contained.

But there's one more twist to this story.

AGAINST ALL ODDS

Those who had witnessed Jesus' return firsthand were busy telling others. It would have been very difficult to contain the excitement. The reports could be verified by anyone in Jerusalem who had been present, and as a result, the news was spreading quickly. Even many Jewish priests came to believe Jesus was the messiah, despite their role in his crucifixion.[14]

Jesus of Nazareth is, in a very real sense, the pivot point of history. Just as Jesus divides the calendar into two halves, he also divides the Bible: the Old Testament preceded his birth, and the New Testament chronicles events that transpired afterward.

During Jesus' lifetime, the Old Testament half was all there was. It was written hundreds of years before he was born. In fact, the first five books are believed to have been recorded by Moses. Jesus affirmed this when he said:

> If you believed Moses, you would believe me, for he wrote about me. But since you do not believe what he wrote, how are you going to believe what I say?[15]

In saying this, Jesus affirmed the accuracy of these writings. And then, soon after his death, burial, and resurrection, the second half was written to deliver the good news: Jesus came to conquer death, and proved his victory when he rose to life and appeared before hundreds of witnesses. The focus of the New Testament is on Jesus of Nazareth, and who he claimed to be.

Consider the following passage:

> I am scorned and despised by all! Everyone who sees me mocks me. They sneer and shake their heads, saying, "Is this the one who relies on the Lord? Then let the Lord save him! If the Lord loves him so much, let the Lord rescue him!"...
>
> My life is poured out like water, and all my bones are out of joint. My heart is like wax, melting within me. My strength has dried up like sunbaked clay. My tongue sticks to the roof of my mouth. You have laid me in the dust and left me for dead.
>
> My enemies surround me like a pack of dogs; an evil gang closes in on me. They have pierced my hands and feet.

> I can count all my bones. My enemies stare at me and gloat. They divide my garments among themselves and throw dice for my clothing.[16]

What a grim picture of sadness and defeat. A gentle spirit crushed by evil men. But there's something truly astonishing about this passage: it is from the book of Psalms, which is found in the *Old* Testament. In other words, this passage was written several hundred years before Jesus was born. Before crucifixion had been invented. Before it could even make any sense.

And this brings us to what is considered by many to be the most compelling evidence of all: Jesus fulfilled predictions recorded centuries before his birth, in ways well outside his control. The number of Old Testament passages that align with his life is far beyond coincidence—it is a statistical impossibility.

Here are a few of the Old Testament messianic prophecies that could only be said to apply to one person in all of history:

- Born to a virgin[17]

- Place of birth would be the town of Bethlehem[18]

- Descendant of Abraham, Jacob, and David[19]

- Would be called the Son of God[20]

- Existed before the world was created[21]

- To be called Lord and Immanuel ("God with us")[22]

- Would be a prophet[23]

- Would be a king[24]

- To begin his ministry in Galilee[25]

- Would perform miracles and heal many people[26]

- Was to enter Jerusalem on a donkey[27]

- Rejected by religious leaders[28]

- Brought back to life; his body would not see corruption[29]

These prophetic allusions to the identity of the messiah were not cherry-picked by Jesus' followers after the fact. Long before his birth, these passages had already been cited in Jewish writings outside of the Old Testament as predictive details that would help identify the Christ—a fact that makes his fulfillment of them all the more significant.

Yet there are many more. At least twenty-nine Old Testament prophecies were fulfilled by Jesus within the twenty-four hours leading up to his crucifixion:[30]

- He would be betrayed by a friend[31]

- Would be sold out for thirty pieces of silver[32]

- The silver would be thrown down in God's house[33]

- He was sold for the same price as the potter's field[34]

- His closest followers would abandon him[35]

- False witnesses would accuse him[36]

- He would stand silent before his accusers[37]

- Would be wounded and bruised[38]

- People would strike him and spit upon him[39]

- He would be mocked[40]

- Would be too weak to carry his own cross[41]

- His hands and feet would be pierced[42]

- Would be crucified with thieves[43]

- He would intercede for those who hurt him[44]

- His own people would reject him[45]

- Would be hated without a cause[46]

- Friends would watch his death from far off[47]

- People would shake their heads at him[48]

- Witnesses would stare upon him[49]

- People would split his garments and gamble for them[50]

- He would suffer thirst[51]

- Offered gall and vinegar to drink[52]

- Would cry out to God[53]

- He would commit his spirit to God[54]

- No bones would be broken[55]

- His heart would burst[56]

- His side would be pierced[57]

- Darkness would fall over the land[58]

- He would be buried in a rich man's tomb[59]

No life in history comes close to mirroring these verses except Jesus of Nazareth. It is impossible to control one's ancestry, birth location, method of execution, and so on. Christ couldn't possibly have orchestrated these events, and his enemies wouldn't have willingly done things to bring them to pass. If possible, they would have tried to thwart their fulfillment.

Old Testament authors, Jewish leaders, and Jesus' followers all thought the messiah would rule *forever*. They had no reason to think he would die right away at the hands of his enemies. But many of these prophetic passages describe Christ's last hours of peril, rife with humiliation and defeat, culminating in death. Who would perceive these disappointing and humiliating depictions to be about an anticipated messiah?

The nature of these particular passages became clear only after these events had transpired. In this way, Jesus fulfilled both types of prophecy: those that were understood to be predictions of the messiah, and those no one realized would apply. They did not expect the messiah to die a demeaning death at the hands of his enemies—yet this is precisely what had been foretold all along.

These are not the only verses in the Old Testament that point conclusively to Jesus as the Christ, but they certainly provide a compelling foundation for further research.[60]

THE ONLY EXPLANATION

The collection of writings that comprise the modern Bible have proven strikingly accurate. Its validity is underscored by the fact that Jesus repeatedly cited many passages, and fulfilled dozens of prophecies in ways that no one saw coming—details that could only be known by God when they were first recorded.

After assessing the historical record and the exceptional events surrounding his life, we must now reach a conclusion. Was Jesus crazy, evil... or God?

The evidence clearly favors Jesus' claim of divinity. Had he been just another cult leader, the history recorded in ancient works would look very different. We would never have heard of a lunatic named Jesus, or a con man from Nazareth. And we definitely wouldn't have reset the calendar year.

The history makes no sense—unless Jesus was God.

But if he was, why did he die? Why didn't Jesus summon a column of fire down from the sky and burn all his enemies up?

CHAPTER 8

DEITY

I do not feel obliged to believe that the same God
who has endowed us with sense, reason, and intellect
has intended us to forgo their use.

— GALILEO GALILEI

J ESUS SAID he was God, yet he was crucified. These two facts seem at odds with one another. How could God be killed? Also, the Bible states that God is invisible, yet Jesus was not. It says God is an eternal deity, yet Jesus was a man born to a woman. And it even describes God as only one being, yet Jesus spoke of God as his "Father." None of this appears to make much sense.

To understand what is going on here, we must consider what cannot be seen. The Bible describes God as a spirit, which is an invisible force. When the wind blows, we see tall blades of grass bow in its presence. We hear it. We feel a tickle as it passes over our skin. Its effects are easily observed even though, like a spirit, we cannot see the wind. The two are so similar that the Hebrew word for spirit is *ruwach*, which also translates to "wind."[1]

The wind is an invisible and impersonal force of nature. And we may be inclined to think of God in the same way—as a deity

uninterested in the day-to-day concerns of those he created—but
the Bible describes our creator as full of passion for us, and deeply
interested in each person's life.

But how can a spirit express himself to us? As material beings,
we are naturally unable to see, feel, hear, or communicate with
God. How, then, do we learn who he is? Or that he even exists?
How might our creator reveal himself to us?

The necessity to bridge this spiritual-material divide is clear:
without a visible or audible representation, man would never
know the identity of his creator. For this reason, God sent forth
an incarnation of himself—the material body of the immaterial
spirit, the physical form of the metaphysical deity—which he
calls "the image of God." The Greek word translated "image" here
is *eikōn*, or simply "icon."[2]

God named this only incarnation of himself the *Son of God*: God
in the person of Jesus Christ. In this way, God came to dwell
among, teach, and serve those he created, through his only Son.
Sadly, those Jesus reached out to specifically mocked his title as
the Son of God while they crucified him on the cross—a most
humiliating outcome.[3]

When God took the physical form of man, he also adopted
our inferior qualities. For example, while a supreme deity is
omnipresent—present everywhere at all times—a man can only
stand in one spot. Jesus, therefore, was constrained to appear in a
single location, within a mortal body. The infinite God embraced
these limitations in order to relate to mankind. This allowed our
creator to be seen, touched, and heard, but also to endure the
painful human experiences we all face. Rather than watching
from afar, unaffected by our plight, God suffered just like us.

Since the Son of God was both fully divine and fully man, he
was subject to the laws of nature, but he was able to defy them
when it suited God's purpose. His miracles and resurrection
were supernatural events resulting from his divinity. Yet Jesus

remained a man, which meant his ministry was limited in time to his human lifespan, in space to his immediate geographical area, and in expression to his works and sermons.

Jesus is the visible image of the invisible God.

ONE GOD

A common misconception is that Jesus came into existence when he was born. However, the Bible makes it clear that the Son of God preexisted before his birth to Mary.[4] God, the only eternal spirit, has always existed and will always exist. That he chose to take the form of man and be born into the human race at a particular point in history did not alter God's nature or appearance.

This explains Jesus' claim that he had seen Abraham, even though their lives were separated by nearly two thousand years.[5] When God appeared before Abram and promised to bless his descendants, he needed a physical, visible form. He did so as Jesus—long before the Son of God was later born to Mary.

The Bible makes it clear that all things were created through Jesus.[6] It is fascinating that God created a physical world in which he himself would become a participant. Ultimately, however, he allowed himself to be put to death in his own universe by the very creatures he gave life.

> He was in the world, and the world was made by him, and the world knew him not. He came unto his own, and his own received him not. (John 1:10–11)

The Bible mentions God the Father, the Son of God, and the Holy Spirit.[7] But how can one single God be all of these? It's hard to say. We often describe ourselves as having a body, spirit, and soul (or mind).[8] These are distinctly different from each other, since the body is not the same as the mind. Yet, at the same time, they are one: both the body and the mind belong to one single person. Similarly, though Jesus is distinctly different from God the Father, they are one and the same.

God may not have the same composition as his creatures, but evidently we are similar. The Bible contains references to God as a father, son, and holy spirit. Each seems to describe a part of God, performing different actions in concert with one another to achieve his will. In an effort to explain this divine mystery, theologians devised a model called the *Trinity*, which describes three uncreated, co-equal, eternally existent parts of the same single deity.[9] This concept is widely accepted among most Christians, though the term itself does not appear in the Bible.[10]

To be clear, the God of the Bible is the only deity. There aren't three. Jesus reiterates this in Mark 12:29. Sure, we'd like it to be simple. If we were to devise our own explanation of how God works it would likely be different, as Greek mythology clearly demonstrates. But the biblical explanation is far more nuanced. Describing the nature of an infinite, all-powerful creator may be like trying to explain the sound of an orchestra to someone who is deaf, even though we've never heard music ourselves.

The details of this divine arrangement are certainly mysterious and beyond our full comprehension. The concept of a single God comprised of different parts provides useful insight into passages that would otherwise appear to make no sense. Consider this:

> If you loved me, you would be glad that I am going to the Father, for the Father is greater than I. (John 14:28 NIV)

Yet elsewhere, Jesus equates himself with the Father:

> I and the Father are one. (John 10:30 NIV)

At first, these two passages would appear to contradict. But in light of the descriptions of God's nature set forth elsewhere, they are brought into perfect harmony. Obviously an incarnation of God is inherently limited by taking on an inferior physical form—yet the Son of God remains one with the Father. Both represent the same deity.

AN EXCLUSIVE OFFER

Most self-proclaimed prophets and messengers have produced new literary works and doctrines which seek to revise or supersede the Bible's contents. However, any movement that alters the message cannot also claim to be based on it.

Biblical writings assert exclusive and final authority, forbidding modification.[11] It is also clear that there is only one incarnation of God, and Jesus Christ is this "one and only son."[12] The Bible prophetically predicted and subsequently confirmed that Jesus is the long-awaited messiah, and he claims he is the way, the truth, and the life—not merely a prophet, but God himself.[13] Jesus has declared himself the final word, such that there can be no more prophets or books apart from him. These claims are at the heart of the Christian faith. At first it may seem too absolute or exclusive, but we must ask ourselves: If Jesus is telling the truth, isn't this what we should expect?

Imagine your friend walks in wearing a cast. You'd ask what happened. Your friend gives three conflicting explanations—a story about tripping on a sidewalk, another about foiling a bank robbery, and finally a grizzly bear attack—then tells you to choose which version you want to believe. Your friend explains, "Your perception is all that matters. Everyone can experience their own reality. Different people can arrive at different truths. So just pick whichever one you like!" At this point you'd probably ask what kind of medication they were given.

This sort of "anything goes" answer is absurd. There is only *one* true story behind a broken arm. That's why you asked; you wanted the truth. And yet some will suggest with a straight face that this is a legitimate approach when addressing the topic of religion. The idea itself is logically bankrupt.

Christianity isn't based on a list of teachings or self-help tips. Jesus didn't offer a twelve-step program to improve ourselves, get out of debt, or stay healthy. If Jesus had merely given pointers for happiness, then perhaps we could just pick a few good ones to follow a formula for living life to the fullest.

That's what most faiths do. Teachings are central to most every world religion. They promote key philosophies, emphasize good works, or lay down strict rules. Their focus is primarily on how a follower lives their life. But belief in Christ doesn't hinge on rules or wise proverbs or the teachings of Jesus; rather, it is about the *history* of Jesus. In this way it is unlike other faiths, which emphasize certain behaviors and rites. Belief in Christ is based entirely on the identity and works of *God*—not the believer.

These beliefs are not made true by virtue of dressing, speaking, voting, or praying a certain way. Further, Christ assures us such efforts earn nothing. The events of the Bible are either true or false, and followers of Christ simply believe they are true.

Had your friend with the broken arm instead admitted the truth—that they tripped over a curb and fell—they could assure you it was true by adding, "No matter what anyone else tells you, that's the way it really happened." Is this closed-minded or intolerant? Certainly not.

If an account is true, we expect it to be authoritative. That's exactly what the Bible asserts in its account of past events, and we are encouraged to verify its authenticity.

IN HIS OWN WORDS

Our concepts of God are shaped by a sense of right and wrong, or what we believe is "good," but our ideas may be flawed. Rather than assuming anything, let's consider what the Bible says of God:

1. *God is eternal.* He self-existed before time began. He was not created, and will always continue to exist.[14]

2. *God is all-knowing.* He is omniscient, which means there is nothing that has happened or will ever happen apart from his knowledge.[15]

3. *God is everywhere.* The spirit of God is omnipresent, and his presence is inescapable.[16]

4. *God is sovereign.* Nothing has ever taken place or will ever take place outside his control.[17]

5. *God is love.* He is benevolent. He tells us that anyone who does not love doesn't know him, because "God is love."[18]

6. *God is just and fair.* His purposes are good. God is righteous and loving towards all.[19]

7. *God is not wicked.* He does not take pleasure in wickedness, and he does not do anything wrong.[20]

8. *God never changes.* God makes it clear that he is always the same, no matter what.[21]

9. *God created everything.* Nothing exists that wasn't willfully created by God.[22]

10. *God made everything for himself.* All things were made by God for his own pleasure.[23]

These self-described characteristics of the creator are much more than merely descriptions. They are also promises.

We might say God can do anything he wants, but that isn't really true. God's description of himself includes things he *cannot* do, such as changing or lying.[24] Taken together, these promises impose restrictions on what we can expect of him. This list of "limitations"—if they can even be called that—are actually what make God great. They form the basis of his benevolence, give us hope, and assure us he will never change.

A child may not fully understand her parents' decisions, but she has come to know what she can expect from them. Hopefully her parents love her and have her best interests in mind, and she can lean on them even when things seem unfair. During tragedy or difficult circumstances, we can take great comfort in relying on someone we trust—someone who has shown that they care.

We tend to worry. We see the troubled world around us, and we wonder who's really in control. God wants all people to trust and rely on him, but in order to do that, we must first know who he is. God has made his identity clear to us as a source of peace and hope: a caring, loving creator who is concerned with every detail of our lives, and who personally came to meet us.

WORTHY OF HONOR

Now let's look at what God *isn't* like: us. Many passages in the Bible seem to personify God with human qualities. For example, in Genesis 3:9, God calls out to Adam in the garden and asks where he is. But wouldn't an omniscient deity already know this?

Of course. It's a bit like playing hide-and-seek with a child: they may giggle and reveal where they are, but we question aloud as we continue our search. This event could have been recorded differently to avoid any misunderstanding about whether God knew Adam's location, but it wasn't. Instead, we are treated to the image of a father who wants to speak with his child. He knows exactly where the child is, yet the father calls out to him, inviting his son to come forth and show himself. It was a chance to bond and, given the context, it was also an opportunity for Adam to admit he'd disobeyed. In any case, this passage wasn't provided to show that God is just like us, or that he really loses us when we hide. Instead, it reveals the distance Adam felt.

Similarly, God is said to "regret" creating man in Genesis 6:6. But how could God regret doing precisely what he chose to do, especially when he knew beforehand what the outcome would be? Passages such as these—in which the deity is said to have had feelings such as jealousy, anger, or change of heart—ascribe the attitudes and emotions of men to the deity to permit understanding for the reader's sake.

Verses like these were not intended to convey God's character, or to suggest that he made a mistake by creating mankind. God's identity is expressly and explicitly stated elsewhere. We should rely on those clear declarations God has made of himself, rather than colorful imagery used in the context of a particular story.

Sadly, many people perceive our creator to be similar to an overbearing boss, watching and waiting for any mistake so he can forcefully and vengefully punish us. Certainly an angry god wielding a fistful of lightning bolts would be feared. But would his actions elicit honor or praise? Love is not the natural reaction to a relentless tyrant. Fear is.

Others struggle to reconcile the extreme violence, suffering, and calamity in this world with a loving God. To set their minds somewhat at ease, some have concluded that although a creator originally designed the universe, he must be an impersonal force that has little interest in our troubles. While at first this seems to excuse the pain we feel, it doesn't help much: that creator is no more worthy of praise than a father who abandons his children.

God tells us he cares. He created us for his own pleasure. He even came to visit us. But if God is good and he loves us, then why is there so much trouble in this life?

Why does God continue to allow us to suffer?

CHAPTER 9

EVIL

*When I despair, I remember that all through history
the way of truth and love have always won. There have
been tyrants and murderers, and for a time, they can seem
invincible, but in the end, they always fall.*

— MAHATMA GANDHI

P AIN AND SUFFERING surround us. People are being subjected
to unspeakable acts of evil each day. We don't enjoy it, and
neither does God. So how did evil get here? And if God doesn't
like it, why does it continue to exist?

It's important to recognize the reason we know the difference
between good and evil. Take light and darkness: If all we'd ever
seen was darkness, we couldn't understand what light is. We
might try to imagine it, but we can never truly appreciate light
or darkness without seeing both. Knowledge of both is required
because it is the contrast between the two that defines each one.
We can't grasp either one until we experience its alternative.

The same is true of good and evil. Without seeing what is bad,
we can't comprehend what it means for something to be good.
Is it possible to truly appreciate one's wealth without knowing
poverty? Or health, having never battled infirmity? Would the

joy of true friendship feel the same to one who had never experienced loneliness? We treasure the greatest gifts in life as a result of this contrast. Only through tasting the duality of both do we become capable of appreciating the joy that follows sorrow.

Imagine a room filled with bright sunlight beaming in through uncovered windows. If you wanted to dim the light a bit, would you turn on a device that emits darkness? Of course not, because darkness is the *absence* of light rather than a presence. The only way to make the room dark would be to block the light, because light is dominant. It will always prevail over darkness.

Evil represents disorder. However, it is not the presence of any particular force. Rather, it is the *absence* of perfection. Evil exists because our world currently lacks the full measure of God's influence. He is light, and in him there is no darkness at all.[1] However, the world he created is home to dark shadows which reveal the deep pain that results from choosing "good enough" over perfection. This present state of disorder allows us to fully comprehend the deplorable alternative to a flawless universe.

The absence of perfection has been temporarily permitted so that God's plan, when finally brought about, can be fully desired, fully appreciated, and fully experienced. Like light, perfection is dominant, and will ultimately prevail. Chaos and darkness will not remain forever.

GOD CREATED EVERYTHING

What if a certain model of vehicle used the left blinker to signal right turns, and the right blinker for left turns? Would this be the driver's fault? Of course not. Is the vehicle to blame? No, it is functioning as expected; someone designed and built it this way. It could have been an oversight, or the engineer may have made a conscious decision. We can blame him for the bad design, but we can hardly blame the machine. Created things don't design themselves.

God tells us he created everything. All things that exist were made by him, including the temporary effects of disorder we see around us. Because pain exists, it must be part of his plan—even if only for a brief time. Since it undoubtedly grieves him, we must conclude that evil plays an important role, otherwise God wouldn't allow it to exist. Perhaps it is essential to giving us the ability to choose our own path.

God tells us he is sovereign over all. This means he has the power to instantly eliminate all evil. Obviously he has chosen not to. So it continues—not merely to exist, but to spread and to operate, despite all the pain it brings. And God knew the future before he created the universe. So regardless of why or how, God was fully aware that evil would eventually make its way into the world. The inescapable conclusion, then, is that God has either

1. directly brought evil into existence; or

2. created beings that he knew would bring evil into existence.

In a moment we'll review the scriptural support for each option, but in the end there is little difference between the two. Regardless of the manner in which evil was introduced, God knew the outcome—and he alone allowed it to happen. (If you find yourself troubled by this idea, you may wish to review the list of God's self-proclaimed characteristics in the previous chapter. Any other conclusion would violate at least two of his promises.)

It seems that some believe the sudden appearance of evil in God's universe was an unforeseen development. Perhaps they imagine God was upset since he thought his creation was perfect, and any disorder was a surprise to him. This is a flagrant denial of both God's sovereignty and his omniscience.

God tells us he is all-powerful and has sovereign authority over everything in the universe. He assures us that nothing takes place outside his control, or without his knowledge. If we are to believe this, then we must conclude that evil exists because God allows it to. Otherwise, if he didn't plan for things to go this way, then who is *really* in control? And what would prevent something similar from happening again in the future? Who has ultimate authority over the universe, if not its creator?

God has evidently permitted evil—the absence of perfection that results in corruption, destruction, and disorder—to come into existence on purpose, and he continues to allow it to exist today. To believe otherwise would contradict this verse:

> For everything comes from him and exists by his power
> and is intended for his glory. (Romans 11:36 NLT)

To be clear, evil itself doesn't bring glory to God. God doesn't delight in wickedness, nor is he the author of it. The declarations concerning his identity expressly assure us that God is incapable of committing wicked acts. God's benevolent nature forces us to conclude that evil's brief presence must ultimately be to our benefit—or else he wouldn't allow it.

THE ORIGIN OF EVIL

Perplexed theologians have struggled for millennia with the notion that God himself would permit evil to exist, so most have instead blamed his creatures. However, attempts to absolve God of any involvement in this matter may be futile. Some verses clearly suggest that God introduced disorder on purpose:

> I form the light, and create darkness: I make peace, and
> create evil: I the Lord do all these things. (Isaiah 45:7)

The word translated *evil* in this passage comes from the Hebrew word *ra*.[2] It is translated this way 442 times in the King James Version, and it is the same word used for the evil that men engage in (Genesis 6:5) and are told to avoid (Psalm 34:14). It represents all types of disorder. In other passages, the same noun is translated *evil*, *distress*, *misery*, *injury*, *calamity*, *adversity*, *wrong*, and *evil* (in an ethical sense).

Of course, many "evils" are not the result of ill intent. Forest fires and earthquakes are examples of natural calamities that God permits. These aren't malicious schemes hatched by wicked men, but simply forces of nature—forces that presently lack order and harmony. In English, *evil* often conveys a malevolent motive, but in its purest sense, it represents anything short of perfection.

God takes no pleasure in evil. His character dictates the terms under which evil is permitted to exist and the constraints it is subject to. Evil isn't here just to complicate our lives for no reason. Indeed, it may be that in order to permit free choice, disorder was *required* to exist—an alternative to perfection to give us the freedom to choose between doing it *God's* way and doing it *our* way. This would make it quite literally a necessary evil, since without another option, we would have no choice at all.

THE ADVERSARY

The Old Testament refers to a creature identified by the Hebrew word *satan*, which means "adversary" or "accuser." This word is a title, but in English it commonly appears as the name Satan. This personification seems appropriate because the adversary demonstrates the ability to communicate and reason intelligently. In the New Testament, the equivalent Greek word is *diabolos*, often translated "devil." This word conjures imagery not found in the Bible; the traditional red skin, horns, hoofed feet, pointed tail and pitchfork are concepts based on pagan mythology.

Satan works against us (1 Peter 5:8). He wields immense power. The whole world is under his control (1 John 5:19). He is referred to as both the prince and god of this world.[3] He has authority over all its kingdoms, which he offered to Jesus on the mountaintop to tempt him—if Jesus would simply fall down and worship him.[4] The adversary is clearly evil. But why? And where did his power and authority come from?

As mentioned before, God either brought evil directly into existence, or created a being he knew would do the same. Let's first review the scriptural support for the traditional view that Satan was originally a sinless being that later chose evil. Second, we'll review verses that suggest God created an adversary that sought only evil from the beginning.

Many Christians teach that Satan was created as a perfect and beautiful angel of light, but he later became prideful and decided to revolt against God. This view rests primarily on four passages. In the first, Luke 10:17–20, Jesus says he saw Satan fall "like lightning" from heaven. The second, Revelation 12:7–13, mentions war in heaven, and Satan being cast out of heaven and into the earth. However, being cast from heaven does not prove that Satan was originally created sinless, as this could occur either way. In addition, the chronology of the passage in Revelation suggests this may be a future event.

Some suggest God can't bear to be in the presence of sin, and offer these passages as proof that Satan was cast from heaven once he became sinful. However, it should be noted that in Job 1:6, Satan comes before God to talk about the evil things he wishes to do to Job—yet he is not cast out of heaven for this. Far from it, actually: God gives him *permission* to attack Job, and imposes limits on the damage Satan is allowed to cause!

The remaining two passages, Isaiah 14:3–17 and Ezekiel 28:11–19, offer the strongest evidence for the view that Satan was once sinless. Each describes a powerful king that became prideful, wished to be like God, and was cast down to the earth. The passage in Ezekiel describes the king as the seal of perfection, full of wisdom and perfect in beauty. It even states that he was an "anointed cherub" in Eden, the garden of God, adorned with precious stones—and that he was blameless in his ways from the day he was created, until wickedness was found in him.

However, neither passage explicitly mentions Satan. In fact, they refer to the kings of Babylon and Tyre, respectively. And both unequivocally state they are references to *a man*. While it is true that few other creatures could be said to be present in Eden, the evidence for this view is far from certain. It requires us to ignore a plain reading of the passage and interpret symbolic imagery as references to a different creature.[5] It relies heavily on the Latin word *lucifer*, which appears in many antiquated translations, but nowhere in the original languages.[6] Satan is usually referred to by the titles found in Revelation 20:2, which are

- the dragon,

- the old serpent,

- the wild beast,

- the devil, or

- the adversary.

Nowhere is Satan referred to as an angel. Quite the opposite, in fact: he is said to masquerade as an "angel of light," which implies he's nothing of the sort.[7] He is distinguished from angels in phrases such as "the dragon and his angels" (Revelation 12:7). Ephesians 2:1–2 describes him as a spirit. But regardless of what *kind* of creature he is, we must confront a bigger question.

DID SATAN CHOOSE EVIL?

It is possible that the "fallen angel" version of Satan's origin story is simply an invention by clever minds in an attempt to absolve God of permitting evil. By imagining a perfect being who somehow later fell into imperfection, they seek to distance this whole mess from God. However, they seem to be unaware of the dilemma this presents: If a being were created *flawless*, how could it ever fall or become corrupted? If God's aim was to create a perfect creature then he certainly failed miserably, because this "perfect angel" has become the bane of the world's existence.

If a creature were truly designed perfect, it would never fail
under any circumstance. It would be purely good—though it
wouldn't have the freedom to make a bad choice.

But what if God created something unlike the rest? What if
he created a being without imparting *any* of his spirit of goodness into it? Without any measure of God's perfection, its only
desire would be to cause disorder. It would also lack freedom of
choice, forever bent on wreaking havoc. Could God do such a
thing? Could he create a beast to visit calamity and discord on an
otherwise peaceful world? It certainly seems possible:

> See, it is I who created the blacksmith who fans the
> coals into flame and forges a weapon fit for its work.
> And it is I who have created the destroyer to wreak
> havoc. (Isaiah 54:16 NIV)

In fact, God's authority is so supreme, his rule so absolute, and his
power so clear to the created, that it's possible no rational creature
would ever have attempted to oppose him... unless it was *deceived*
or *designed to*. Perhaps God uses the adversary to give the rest of
his creation a choice between perfection and its only alternative:
rejecting God.

It is difficult, to say the least, to reconcile the traditional teaching of a sinless angel with verses like this:

> You belong to your father, the devil, and you want to carry
> out your father's desires. He was a murderer from the
> beginning, not holding to the truth, for there is no truth
> in him. When he lies, he speaks his native language, for
> he is a liar and the father of lies. (John 8:44 NIV)

Lies are the adversary's *native* language. He was crooked *from
the beginning*. Mankind is also flawed, to be sure—but can you
imagine if the same statements were made of man? Adam was
never called a liar or a murderer from the beginning. Man was
never said to have no truth in him. These statements are unique

to Satan, whose name literally means "adversary." Adam wasn't named *Enemy*. Further, the adversary appears to be distinguished from other acts of creation:

> By his spirit he hath garnished the heavens; his hand hath formed the crooked serpent. (Job 26:13)

The original Hebrew word translated "crooked" means *fleeing* or *fugitive*.[8] This certainly suggests the adversary was on the run the instant it was made, and was not at peace with God. Other acts of creation are described in harmony with the spirit of God, but this unique creature appears to have been forged by his hand, at arm's length—perhaps out of necessity. Whereas Adam was formed from the dust and then had the spirit of God breathed into him, the crooked serpent was simply formed.[9] What if every element of creation was endowed with the goodness of God through his spirit, except for this one?

While these passages seem fairly conclusive, Revelation 20:10 describes Satan's future judgment. It seems unjust for God to punish Satan for doing or becoming what he intended, unless he had a choice in the matter. Adam chose to gain the knowledge of good and evil. It's possible that Satan was given a choice too, but rather than choosing to *know* good and evil, he chose which one to *become*—such that the choice changed his very constitution, resulting in a new creature incapable of good. Still, choosing an option means it already exists... so we find ourselves struggling once again to explain the origin of evil, and pressed to answer how Satan himself was tempted.

GOD IS IN CONTROL

No matter what conclusions we may draw from the sum of these verses, God says he created everything. Everything exists by his power—including the adversary and all the pain of his deception. If God had not permitted evil to exist or operate, everything in the universe might well be in a state of absolute, robotic perfection. Free choice may not otherwise exist, and we wouldn't have the freedom to either accept or reject our creator.

Whether God introduced the adversary directly or the adversary chose to revolt, God alone designed him and knew what the result would be. God certainly doesn't need our help absolving him of anything. The adversary serves a purpose. His inception didn't bring the creator any joy, but his existence will eventually accomplish God's grand goal of multiplying ours. And though it troubles us now, the work of the destroyer will bring about a more celebrated outcome in the end.

Many scholars believe one-third of God's celestial beings—or angels—chose to follow Satan's lead, granting him much greater influence on earthly affairs.[10] Despite his tremendous power, the adversary must operate within constraints imposed by God.[11] When Satan asked for God's approval to sift Peter "like wheat," it was granted.[12]   Satan also requested God's permission to devastate Job—and received it.[13] We must remember that even after Job lost everything, he "did not sin by charging God with wrongdoing." Neither should we. God himself doesn't perpetrate the wicked designs of the adversary, but it's undeniable that he permits them to happen.

If God had created the universe absolutely perfect, there would be no pain, no death, no suffering. This obviously isn't the case. While perfection is God's *ultimate* goal, we clearly aren't there yet. Imperfection exists now because God allows it to. Not only does he state this unequivocally, it's the only explanation that makes sense if we truly believe that God is in complete control.

The entrance of disorder into the universe was no accident. It did not surprise God or occur outside his will. It was deliberately permitted to exist, and its consequences felt.

Everything is going according to plan.

CHAPTER 10

IMPERFECTION

We must question the story logic of having an all-knowing
all-powerful God, who creates faulty humans, and then
blames them for his own mistakes.

— GENE RODDENBERRY

T HE CREATION NARRATIVES found in many ancient writings
contain striking similarities to the account set forth in the
Bible. The book of Genesis describes creation in a seven-day story.
Each day, God reflected on his work and saw that it was good. But
on day six, God created man in his own image—and said it was
very good.[1] Our creator takes great pride in us.

We were created in the image of the creator, modeled after Jesus.
Just as a father looks at his child and is filled with joy, our creator
looks upon mankind and sees the likeness of the Son of Man—and
he is very pleased. God values each and every one of us.

Adam and Eve, the original two ancestors of all mankind, were
created by God and placed in the Garden of Eden. There, the
pre-incarnate Jesus befriended them, walked with them, and
gave them food to enjoy. He even gave them dominion over his
creation and allowed Adam to name all the animals.

It doesn't get much better than that, but Adam and Eve were naïve. They had no idea how good things were, because they knew nothing other than peace, love, abundance, and joy.

God had no intention for things to stay this way. The Bible says he had placed a special tree in the midst of the garden, and commanded Adam and Eve not to eat from it. How long could they resist? Years? Days? We aren't told. What we do know is that they didn't simply disobey on their own. The adversary was permitted to enter the garden to deceive Eve into taking the one single action God had forbidden:

> Now the serpent was more crafty than any other beast of the field that the Lord God had made. He said to the woman, "Did God actually say, 'You shall not eat of any tree in the garden'?"
>
> And the woman said to the serpent, "We may eat of the fruit of the trees in the garden, but God said, 'You shall not eat of the fruit of the tree that is in the midst of the garden, neither shall you touch it, lest you die.'"
>
> But the serpent said to the woman, "You will not surely die. For God knows that when you eat of it your eyes will be opened, and you will be like God, knowing good and evil."
>
> So when the woman saw that the tree was good for food, and that it was a delight to the eyes, and that the tree was to be desired to make one wise, she took of its fruit and ate, and she also gave some to her husband who was with her, and he ate. Then the eyes of both were opened, and they knew that they were naked. And they sewed fig leaves together and made themselves loincloths.[2]

Not only did God place this beautiful tree full of attractive fruit well within reach, but he also allowed an enemy into the garden to mislead his beloved creatures. Adam and Eve were not equipped with the wisdom or fortitude to resist such temptation. In fact,

God called it "the tree of the knowledge of good and evil," which indicates Adam and Eve understood neither.[3]

Obviously we weren't created perfect, or else we wouldn't have disobeyed. And neither were we created evil. We were created in the image of God, but the freedom of choice leaves us susceptible to circumstance. Perhaps, left only in the company of our perfect creator, we never would have eaten from the tree... but that's not what happened.

In gaining this knowledge, God's plan was set in motion. Without it, Adam and Eve would have remained unable to grasp the contrast between perfection and chaos, and could never truly understand the blessings bestowed upon them by their creator.

Eve was deceived, but Adam was not. He made a deliberate choice to become enlightened. He chose to know what good and evil are, just as we would have done. Mankind chose this path, and that's exactly what God expected.

ACCORDING TO PLAN

Many modern Christian teachers and resources seem to suggest that Adam and Eve were created flawless in a perfect utopia, and that they ruined God's plan by eating from the wrong tree. As a result, God is scrambling to recover from this unforeseen mess, and doing his best to save as many people as he can from the clutches of the adversary.

But that's nonsense. God isn't struggling to return us back to the way things were in Eden. It wouldn't benefit us to be restored to ignorance. Rather, his plan has always been for us to learn from our choices. Disobeying God did not please him, but his plan was to permit that choice anyway, and use it to our benefit.[4]

We know that no one is perfect, and that everyone has made bad decisions. Adam had the freedom to choose, but in reality, it couldn't have turned out any other way. Why? Because God has subjected all of us to disorder—not by our choice, but by *his* will:

> For the creation was subjected to frustration, not by its
> own choice, but by the will of the one who subjected it,
> in hope that the creation itself will be liberated from its
> bondage to decay and brought into the freedom and glory
> of the children of God. (Romans 8:20–21 NIV)

Man's decision to deviate is a necessary element of God's plan. Just as a child's resolve would eventually crumble before a jar of cookies, Adam's choice was inevitable.

This decision did not create evil. The crooked serpent existed prior to Adam's fall. We merely gained the *knowledge* of good and evil, which enabled Adam to see the contrast between his former paradise and the new world of disorder in which we now live.

Our subjection to frustration requires us to experience it fully. The consequences of evil can be partially mitigated by making better choices, but its sting is always felt—even when we try to do things right. No one can escape the clutches of disorder.

As with any good lie, the adversary's pitch contained elements of truth. As promised, Adam became "like God" in knowing good and evil.[5] The adversary's claim that Adam would not die seemed to have some validity. Though he did not die immediately, he immediately *began* to die. His body, previously protected, started to age and decay. Death entered the human race through Adam. As a result, every one of his descendants—everyone who ever lived—is dying or dead.

Once they disobeyed, God banished Adam and Eve from the garden. What may appear to be a harsh penalty is actually the response of a loving father: Genesis tells us there was another tree present in the garden—the tree of life—and its fruit would sustain Adam and Eve perpetually. Had they subsequently eaten from it, their lives would have been extended, along with the length of their curse. Death, however unwelcome, eventually brought an end to their struggle. God would not permit Adam's affliction to continue indefinitely, so he removed them from the garden and placed a guard near the tree of life to block access to it. For the man who had previously inhabited a paradise in which he walked with God, things were looking quite bleak.

MISSING THE MARK

When a marksman takes aim at the center of a target but hits outside the bullseye, we say he missed. No one is a perfect shot every time.

Adam's efforts fell short of perfection too. His condition was somewhat beyond his control, because if God had wanted him to be perfect, he could have created Adam that way—but he didn't. So, despite a desire to do the right thing, he found himself making poor choices. That's what imperfection looks like. It can be something as contemptible as theft, deceit, or murder, but it also includes anything as minor as a mistake, an oversight, or a missed target.[6] And that's exactly what *sin* means in the original language: a miss.[7] Sin represents anything short of perfection.

Even with rigorous training, a dog remains a dog, and it will always be tempted to follow its tendencies. Likewise, we can't simply decide to be perfect. We will continue to make poor choices despite our best efforts because disorder prevails. Our temptations come not from God, but from the evil that surrounds us.[8] While the adversary has the power to focus his destructive efforts on anyone he chooses, there is little need. In our weakened condition, we're already pretty good at messing things up without any help. All of us have made mistakes.[9]

I'm not so bad, you may think. That's true. Or maybe you think, *But I've done so many terrible things*. Perhaps so. Regardless, we were made in God's image. He looked upon us and saw that his design was "very good." This goodness is in our nature.

All men are equipped with an innate sense of what is right, even if we choose to ignore it. Additionally, Adam's choice gave us the knowledge of good and evil, which is evident in the justification we perform in our own minds. We still make selfish decisions, but we're ready with an excuse, a reason, an explanation for our behavior—to make it sound *good*—because even in this wayward age, the most evil schemes concocted by men must be disguised as something good in order to be accepted.

In every society, people repeatedly fail to adhere to their own standards. Each culture draws different boundaries on acceptable behavior, yet no matter where these limits are established, they will be violated. Someone will always be in prison. We cannot live up to our own flimsy standards—let alone perfection.

Even the most intelligent animals cannot comprehend good and evil. They may have protective instincts, feel emotions, or be trained to behave in certain ways that mimic our values, but they cannot perceive morality. This ability is exclusive to mankind. We have been made in the image of God and given the knowledge of good and evil so that now, like God, we see.

The Bible states that the wages of sin is death.[10] In other words, imperfection results in the end of life. By God's gracious design, dying culminates in death, and dying will not last forever. The alternative—suffering the effects of evil and decay *indefinitely*—is truly unimaginable.

As the first man, Adam's body contained the seed of all mankind, and every descendant that has ever lived was inside him the moment he sinned.[11] Consequently, we all shared in his choice and its consequence. Even though he was one man, and even though he alone made the choice, we all sinned when Adam did. As a result, a death sentence was conferred to every person:

> Therefore, just as sin entered the world through one man, and death through sin, and in this way death came to all people, because all sinned. (Romans 5:12 NIV)

Eve was deceived by the adversary. But Adam, who was torn between following God or the companion he loved, made a deliberate choice to defy God's command. Adam was held responsible for this offense, which sentenced mankind to mortality.[12]

From our first breath, we are already enslaved to sin and death.[13] Adam's sin, his death sentence, and the knowledge of good and evil were imputed to every person, without any action on our part. Why must we suffer for a choice our ancestor made? It may seem unfair, but this is how life works. Decisions are not made in isolation, and they invariably affect everyone around us. The decisions of a father can make his child's life wonderful... or hell on earth.

There is nothing unjust in allowing a choice between good and evil. Adam had his. We have our own every day. These decisions have an enormous impact. It might seem unfair at first, but in reality, if God were to intervene and protect us (or others) from our poor choices, it would impinge on our freedom to choose. It would limit what we learn. This is obviously not God's plan. Instead we are allowed to make our own choices—and then we must fully reap the consequences.

MAN VERSUS SELF

Of the body, spirit, and soul, the body is readily observed as the weakest component. The Bible refers to the body of mankind as the *flesh*. It requires food and water each day, sleep each night, and shelter from the elements.

The impact Adam's sin had on our spirit or soul may be more difficult to quantify, but the body provides tangible outward evidence of decay and death. We hunger and thirst. We grow tired, ill, frail. The body itself, in this weakened state, drives us to make poor choices. Though we now know good and evil, we still can't see clearly. The fear of death and the pain of life influence our actions. We search for security and comfort. We succumb to self-indulgent impulses. In our weakness, we seek to gratify ourselves rather than do what we know is best. As Paul put it:

> For I know that nothing good dwells in me, that is, in my
> flesh. For I have the desire to do what is right, but not the
> ability to carry it out. For I do not do the good I want, but
> the evil I do not want is what I keep on doing.[14]

Our bondage to decay and death is not something we can opt out of. It is unnatural and unwanted, but inherited and inescapable.

A world-class athlete cannot accept mediocrity, and always strives for excellence. And yet God has set the bar even higher: *perfection*. But this goal is at odds with our condition. One single mistake makes it unattainable forever, and the corruption we are enslaved to lies outside our control. Adam's sin resulted in separation from God.[15] Remember when God was calling out for Adam and seeking him in the garden? God didn't abandon Adam after he made his mistake. But the guilt and shame Adam brought upon himself introduced a barrier for him that prevented Adam from approaching his Father the way he had before.

God loves us very much. He does not want to be separated from us. However, we can't simply undo what has already happened. We're far from perfect, and because of that, we're stuck running from God instead of embracing him. How can we fix this?

We can't.

CHAPTER 11

POWER

As truly as God by His power once created, so truly
by that same power must God every moment maintain.

— ANDREW MURRAY

N OTHING takes God by surprise. He knows the beginning
from the end. There is no "Plan B." By definition, there can
be only *one* sovereign authority, and he is it.[1] If this weren't true,
then something else—some outside force—could exercise control
over God. If anything else were powerful enough to usurp God's
authority, then it would be a greater power than he, and it should
be revered instead.

Of course, with such complete control comes great responsibility. God designed and created the universe and all that exists
within it, including the adversary. He is the owner of all things,
and he alone is responsible for the well-being of every member of
his creation. Though our eyes are clouded and our judgment fails
us, he sees our condition with perfect clarity, and knows what
must be done to correct it.

The truth is that we cannot do anything to change our situation.
Only God has the power to fix it, and he makes this clear:

> For God has bound everyone over to disobedience so that
> he may have mercy on them all. (Romans 11:32 NIV)

God did what? That's right. And we're totally dependent on him.

MAKING THINGS RIGHT

When we do something wrong, we may feel a bit of guilt. We might try to fix the problem, or even do something charitable for someone else, in an effort to put things back in order.

If we miss the mark, including when we deliberately injure another person, the offense is actually committed against God. God grieves most when we choose disorder because he is actively inviting us to enjoy something better. We might be forgiven by those we've hurt, but ultimately only God's forgiveness matters, because the creator alone judges his creation.

After breaking the one and only rule in the Garden of Eden, Adam and Eve's eyes were opened to good and evil. Realizing they were naked, they immediately sought to cover themselves with clothing made of fig leaves.[2] But God, before removing them from the garden, took it a step further:

> The LORD God made garments of skin for Adam and his
> wife and clothed them. (Genesis 3:21 NIV)

Adam and Eve directly violated God's only rule and they deserved punishment. Instead, God took the life of one of his own animals to make clothes for them. They didn't ask for or deserve this favor. They didn't realize the importance of having protective clothing to guard them from the world outside the garden yet. But his love for those he created led God to sacrifice an innocent creature to cover them—both literally and figuratively.

Religious animal sacrifices are uncommon today, but long ago there was a period of time when it was required of the Israelites. Ancient laws prescribed these offerings because the consequence of sin is death, without which there could be no forgiveness of sins.[3] This practice allowed man to acknowledge utter reliance on God for everything: the blameless offering slain, the mercy sought, and the life only he can give. More importantly, the ritual itself looked forward to a time when God would provide a final solution to the dilemma introduced by Adam's choice.

Today, animal sacrifices are no longer warranted since God has already provided everything for us, similar to the way he helped Adam and Eve. And this brings us to the crux of Christianity.

THE ONLY CURE

Sin rages on. It is clear that the death and devastation visited upon humanity cannot be fixed with a snap of our fingers. We can't simply choose to live forever, nor to behave perfectly.

Perfection is impossible once the very first mistake is made. If the first answer on an exam is wrong, it doesn't matter if the last ninety-nine are right. Doing our best on all the other questions will never yield a perfect score. Likewise, finishing out our lives with perfect decisions cannot undo a single poor one, including Adam's first mistake. There are no works, deeds, or actions we can take to free ourselves from the clutches of sin and death.

Adam's choice to defy God plunged all mankind into darkness and despair. Despite the devastating damage this caused, it was not the most awful atrocity committed by mankind.

No, we did something far worse.

When God introduced himself to us as Jesus Christ, we hated him. We put a crown of thorns on his head, spat on him, mocked him, beat him nearly to death, stripped him naked, nailed him to a post, cursed him, let him die a slow and painful death, and then finished him off with a spear to the side. The same men Jesus created spilled his blood on the earth he designed for them. This is, without a doubt, mankind's most shameful decision.

Was God grieved? Sure. But he wasn't surprised. In fact—and this is amazing—it *pleased* God to crush his only son, because in doing so, his will was being carried out.[4] Now, how could this possibly be what God wanted?

In committing this evil deed, mankind unwittingly sacrificed Christ, the sinless image of God. This allowed Jesus, the ultimate sacrifice, to take the burden of all mankind's imperfections and iniquities on himself. Jesus offered his sinless life to undo all of mankind's failures. This is why Jesus is referred to as "the Lamb of God, who takes away the sin of the world."[5] This is the way God chose to rid the world of sin, defeat death, and reconcile his creatures to himself. And it is a solution only he could provide.

As Jesus hung from the cross, the sin of the entire world was transferred to him.[6] The world—whose sins should result in not merely dying, but *permanent death*—had all its mistakes taken away and placed on Christ. In his final moments on the cross Jesus uttered, "It is finished."[7] He immediately gave up his spirit and died. With this, the ransom to free mankind from its bondage to sin and death was paid in full. The sinless life of Christ culminated in this final, righteous choice.

It is finished.

Jesus' blood was given to remove the mistakes of all people, analogous to the animal sacrifices once decreed by God. The old symbolic practice of killing an innocent animal foreshadowed this event in which the perfect sacrifice was made once and for all, to fully and finally take away every sin ever to be committed.[8]

In his infinite wisdom, God used Adam's poor decision in the garden for a good purpose: to give us deeper understanding, to reveal our imperfections, and to show the stark contrast between our standards and his own.

In the same way, God has masterfully converted the pinnacle of our evil acts—the brutal murder of his only Son—into the greatest blessing of all.[9] In what appears to be a divine checkmate, God turned our detestable choice to nail Jesus to the cross into the very cure we so desperately need.

FOR GOD SO LOVED THE WORLD

Mankind, created in the image of God, was originally sinless. God gave man the freedom to choose, but warned that breaking his only rule would result in death. God allowed an adversary he had created to tempt man, and man chose to violate God's rule in order to become like God and understand good and evil. All of mankind inherited this sinful condition, which carries a death sentence. Man can do nothing—including good works—to overcome sin or death. To correct the problem, God sacrificed himself to free mankind from its bondage to sin and death.

God is in complete control, and is making everything work out as he pleases. An omnipotent, omniscient God cannot be taken by surprise. Before anything was even created, God knew the end result. He wanted us to have the freedom to choose, but he knew we would fall short of perfection, and that we could never undo that choice to escape the consequences.

The Bible indicates the lamb was slain "from the foundation of the world" because the perfect sacrifice was secured long ago.[10] Before we made our choice—before we even existed—God already had a plan to cure us. He didn't come here to tell us how badly we'd failed, or to condemn us for our poor choices. He came to help us:

> For God so loved the world that he gave his one and only Son, that whoever believes in him shall not perish but have eternal life. For God did not send his Son into the world to condemn the world, but to save the world through him. (John 3:16–17 NIV)

God, seeing that mankind would benefit from the knowledge of good and evil, has allowed sin and death to plague our existence temporarily. Without subjection to disorder, we could never fully appreciate the perfection only he can bring about. Fortunately, this learning period will one day end.

A Christian is someone who relies on Jesus to heal and to give new life in the same way Christ was resurrected. The believer's faith is placed not in his own actions, but in God's. Our efforts contribute nothing to what Jesus accomplished.

But wait, who will benefit from God's selfless sacrifice? How do we know whether we're included?

CHAPTER 12

OPTIONS

*To judge from the notions expounded by
theologians, one must conclude that God created
most men simply with a view to crowding hell.*

— MARQUIS DE SADE

I T IS widely held among world religions that the vast majority
of mankind will be subjected to endless torment after death in
a fiery place they call *hell*, while only a select group is destined
for a paradise called *heaven*. Isn't it curious that everyone who
believes this way thinks they're on the heaven-bound team?

There is little contention about the existence of paradise in the
afterlife. However, some think the number of people who end up
there will be extremely small, while others think most will make it.
No matter where this line of division is drawn, there is a general
consensus that some will be in heaven, while others remain in
hell forever. But the *number* of people in paradise isn't the focus
of much debate: What really generates controversy is the *criteria*
God will use to decide who ends up where.

Theologians have pondered the question for centuries. Is God's
decision to save certain members of humanity a random drawing?

Is it determined by the choices we make within our brief lifetime? Is it the ratio of good deeds to evil deeds? Whether we kept all Ten Commandments? How much money we gave to charity? Whether we joined the correct church?

This is not a decision to be made lightly. Regardless of whether we are willing to confront this uncomfortable question or not, God must decide each person's fate. Where will he draw the line?

TWO CAMPS

God's criteria for sending some to heaven—and the others to hell—is called the question of *election*. It is the process of sorting who goes where. Most Christians answer this question in one of two ways. Oddly, these two widely accepted mainstream teachings are incompatible and mutually exclusive.

In the 17th century, two influential theologians named John Calvin and Jacobus Arminius championed opposing views on election. These men were deeply divided on who Jesus came to save. Calvin promoted a concept referred to as *unconditional* election, while Arminius held to *conditional* election. Virtually every modern Christian can be categorized as either "Calvinist" or "Arminian," even if they haven't heard these terms, and even if they don't know what election is.

Calvin's view of unconditional election states that Jesus Christ's sacrifice only saves a select group of people, and that God's choice as to who benefits is essentially a lottery: there is no action on our part—good or bad—that has any effect. It is completely unconditional. Some are to be saved and delivered to paradise, while the rest are sent to burn in hell forever. The resulting stark contrast between God's treatment of each group is provided as a not-so-subtle everlasting reminder of how much God loves those he saved... and how much he hates the damned.[1]

If you find that theory a bit unsettling, you're not alone. Many Christians find the thought of such an outcome repulsive. Maybe that's because we're made in the image of God, and if it were up to us, we would at least *try* to save everyone. This is probably why many Christians have embraced the opposing view of conditional election, or Arminianism, which states that Jesus' sacrifice on the cross was for all people rather than just a small group. While the offer to be saved is extended to everyone, salvation depends on one's reaction to the gift, hence the "conditional" part: those who accept the offer go to heaven, and those who reject it are cast into hell and tormented forever.

Which of these two views is correct? The Scriptures appear to support both. There are several verses which, when taken alone, seem to affirm each position. Proponents of unconditional election say men have no choice in the matter because salvation is predetermined, as shown in verses like this:

> You did not choose me, but I chose you and appointed you so that you might go and bear fruit—fruit that will last—and so that whatever you ask in my name the Father will give you. (John 15:16 NIV)

This suggests the afterlife is like a random lottery in which the winning (and losing) numbers have already been drawn. But many Christians oppose this view, and say we *do* have a choice. They point to verses such as:

> Turn to me and be saved, all the ends of the earth! For I am God, and there is no other. (Isaiah 45:22 ESV)

Why would God say this if a select group had already been chosen for paradise, and nothing could be done to change it? If this were true, a person's choice to turn to God would have no effect.

There are *many* other passages in the Bible that lend support to both conditional and unconditional election, which is why these views have been at odds for centuries. Both have valid scriptural support, and both contain elements of truth—yet they completely contradict one another. This seems odd, to say the least. Are these two views the only possibilities?

TWO QUESTIONS, FOUR OPTIONS

Every binary yes-or-no question has only two valid answers. When offered a drink, your answer is either *yes* or *no*. The result is one of two outcomes: either you get a drink, or you don't.

Now let's add one more yes-or-no question, for a total of two. Here's an example. Imagine we've just finished dinner at a nice restaurant, and the waiter brings coffee and creamer to the table. Now you must decide:

- Would you like coffee—yes or no?

- Would you like creamer—yes or no?

Because we've added another question, the number of possible results has now doubled. That means our answers to these two questions will lead to being served one of exactly four possible outcomes:

1. Nothing at all

2. Black coffee

3. Coffee with creamer

4. Just creamer

It's that simple. And while our last option may not sound so good, it is still a possibility!

BIGGER DECISIONS

Our creator must make choices too, and they will have enormous consequences. The possible outcomes, however, are just as easy to quantify. In order to determine who God will allow into heaven, we only need to consider two very simple yes-or-no questions:

- Does God have the *power* to save us all?

- Does God have the *desire* to save us all?

They may seem a little strange, but the answers to these two simple questions will ultimately determine the fate of mankind. And as before, there are exactly four possible options:

1. God has the power, but doesn't want to save us all

2. God wants to, but doesn't have the power to save us all

3. God has neither the power nor the desire to save us all

4. God has both the power and the desire to save us all

Setting all the clouded theology aside, this is where you end up. Every Christian concept of the afterlife will fall within one of these outcomes. These are the only four options available, and exactly one of them must be true.

Recall the two types of election, unconditional and conditional. These are represented by the first two options. The Calvinist view of unconditional election (a lottery) is option one: a God who has the power to save all people but does not want to, so he picks winners and losers. Such a horrific outcome would clearly violate both God's loving nature and any semblance of justice. While it seems to be supported by certain passages, this view contradicts verses that unequivocally express God's desire to save all.[2] There can be no question that God wants all people to be saved because we are specifically told to pray for this outcome.[3]

Next, the view of conditional election—far more popular among modern Christians—is represented by the second option: a God who wants to save everyone, but lacks the authority since man's free will prevents it. Put differently, God *wants* to save us, but our choice limits his power to do so, as it would violate our freedom to choose.[4] This view also seems supported by certain passages. However, it denies God's sovereign authority over *every* power in the universe. In fact, we are expressly assured that no plan of God's can be thwarted.[5] Is this not clearly the most important plan God will ever carry out? Is it this easy for God's creatures to derail his will and render him powerless?

The third option represents a creator who lacks both the power and the desire to save everyone: a weak God who doesn't even care. This view denies both God's desire *and* his power to save all men—a clear violation of all the scriptures marshaled in support of the first two options. It suffers from both of the previous two flaws at the same time, resulting in the same tragic outcome for God's creatures that so desperately need his help.

This leaves one last option. Like ordering a cup of creamer, it is rarely considered. It is unknown to many followers of Christ, and ignored by many modern teachers of organized religion. Yet it is the only logical option that puts these seemingly contradictory scriptures in perfect harmony.

And given what we know about God, it is the only outcome that makes sense.

CHAPTER 13

VICTORY

Darkness cannot drive out darkness; only light can do that.
Hate cannot drive out hate; only love can do that.

— MARTIN LUTHER KING, JR.

J ESUS made it clear that he is the only path to God. He said, "I am the way and the truth and the life. No one comes to the Father except through me."[1] Only Jesus lived a sinless life, was killed, and rose again to conquer sin and death.[2]

Death can't be cured through good behavior. That makes Jesus the one and only hope for mankind to be freed from its bondage to decay. Our fate rests squarely on him. Can he do it?

- Jesus was sent to be "the savior of the world."[3]

- Jesus said he would "draw all people" to himself.[4]

- Jesus prayed for the salvation of all, and his will is to save everyone.[5]

Are these things true? Or will Jesus fail?

Most people I've met believe Christ will fail spectacularly. Not for them, of course, but for everyone else. Today most modern

Christians teach that God lacks either the power or the desire to save us all. They tell us Jesus will *not* succeed in achieving his stated purpose, and that some people will unfortunately slip through the cracks and be lost forever.

I disagree.

After much careful consideration, I believe the Bible clearly and explicitly teaches that *everyone* will eventually enter into a life of peace in paradise with the Creator. God says he loves each of us without fail, and he has both the desire *and* the power to save all people. I believe that ultimately the redemptive work of Christ on the cross will be revealed to all, all will embrace the truth, and all will be reconciled to God. The Scriptures make it crystal clear that sin and death will be *destroyed*, even though modern Christianity denies God's ability to deliver on this promise. I now believe that all people will be released from their captivity to sin, freed from death's grip, and reunited with their loved ones. This won't be instantaneous—and some won't get out easy—but in the end, absolute and total victory for God is guaranteed.

The following chapters reveal the basis for this conclusion, which is stated literally and unequivocally throughout the Bible, hidden in plain sight. My prayer is that you'll truly give this possibility the consideration it deserves. This is a discussion we cannot ignore. It isn't inconsequential. It isn't a matter of opinion. It isn't merely a detail. It is central to God's claim of victory. It is critical to understanding his identity. And in the end, it doesn't matter what we've been told. It is simply a matter of fact: *What do the Scriptures say?*

Some self-proclaimed believers in Christ may take issue with this view, even before weighing the evidence. This is unsurprising: Those already steeped in flawed religious teachings will have a tougher time accepting evidence that challenges their long-held belief in endless torment. I realize the journey out of that dark forest can be unnerving because I walked it too.

For some, it may even feel blasphemous to question concepts parroted for years by demagogues and lay leaders. But for newcomers—those whose minds are not yet clouded with traditions of men—a complete victory for Christ is obvious: it is the only logical outcome to expect if we are to take God at his word.

Sadly, in talking to many devout Christians, one almost gets the feeling that they *want* others to burn in fiery torment forever. I find it difficult to believe that Jesus feels the same way.

WHAT LOSING LOOKS LIKE

Consider the modern popular teaching. We'll even be generous, and say that God saves most people but loses a handful to the adversary in endless hell. Not many, just a few. But no matter where the line of division is drawn, we now have a huge problem: any outcome in which the spoils of mankind are split among two powers—a good God and an evil adversary—equates to *dualism* rather than monotheism. Many Christians mistakenly teach that these two powers will coexist forever, but the Scriptures make it clear that only *one* authority reigns supreme: God.

If the adversary can steal just one person from God's plan to save all, then what is to prevent him from taking more? And if he can take a few, why not all? But God will not have his plan foiled by members of his own creation. The suggestion that God's authority is shared with or thwarted by another power is rank heresy. Oddly, this idea that a powerful adversary will forever taunt God has become a mainstream view among those who claim to believe in the God of the Bible.

Such an outcome is hard to imagine. God, who despises sin, would have to be willing to rope off a portion of his universe to let it reign endlessly; a place of unspeakable anguish designed to forever torment members of his own creation. This would be akin to a father who builds a torture chamber inside his home for his mentally ill wife to punish his children for their behavior...

endlessly. He has complete control, and chooses to relegate it to a confined space—but stuffing evil in its own room is by no means victory over it. It still exists, it still torments his loved ones, and it still remains in power. Authority is split between himself and the evil he hates. Until this blight is destroyed, the man of the house cannot possibly be considered a victor—or even in control.

THE GOOD NEWS

How could it ever be considered victorious for God to topple the adversary, but leave those deceived by him in torment forever? Partial victory is a total failure. Common sense tells us God could never be pleased with this outcome. More importantly, the Bible tells us that God wants *all* people to be saved:

> For this is good and acceptable in the sight of God our Saviour; Who will have *all* men to be saved, and to come unto the knowledge of the truth. For there is one God, and one mediator between God and men, the man Christ Jesus; Who gave himself a ransom for *all*, to be testified in due time. (1 Timothy 2:3–6, *emphasis added*)

God is clear about his plans. And we know he works all things according to his will.[6] His authority is supreme and nothing can stand in his way, so why not win the heart of every man?

While God certainly has the power to do so, he's not going to save anyone by force. It will be more amazing—and useful—for people to see the damage caused by their choices, be rehabilitated, and then gladly choose the winning team. Healing and helping people is exactly what Jesus spent his time doing, and it is difficult to imagine a more glorious end result.

The modern creed teaches that man has until his last breath to decide whether to confess that Jesus is the Son of God, and if he fails to do so, he will awaken to everlasting torment with no hope of escape. His fate, we are told, is then sealed forever. But this presents a number of issues. For example, multitudes of people lived and died without placing their faith in (or even hearing the name of) Jesus. This includes every person mentioned in the Old Testament. King David is described as a man after God's own heart, yet he never even knew the name of the coming messiah, because he lived well before Jesus' time.[7] The Bible plainly states that no one can come to God except by calling on Jesus—so is David burning in hell? Surely not.

God has a plan for everyone. Every individual will be given the opportunity to learn who Jesus is and the price he paid to restore them to life. God's absolute triumph in winning over every heart is assured in verses like this:

> "Turn to me and be saved, all you ends of the earth; for I am God, and there is no other. By myself I have sworn, my mouth has uttered in all integrity a word that will not be revoked: Before me *every* knee will bow; by me *every* tongue will swear. They will say of me, 'In the Lord alone are deliverance and strength.'" *All* who have raged against him will come to him and be put to shame. (Isaiah 45:22–24 NIV, *emphasis added*)

Surely this promise is among the most forceful in the Bible. God guarantees that at some point *every single person* will participate in this. The Hebrew words rendered "swear" (*shaba*) and "bow" (*kara*) mean to take an oath and to lower oneself in reverence, respectively. These are not the actions of depraved or rebellious people, nor is this forced submission—these are confessions that take place only after one has come to the truth and voluntarily embraced it.[8] At some point far in the future, every single knee will bow and every single tongue will confess the truth in a way that brings glory to God. We are even promised that those who spent their time on earth raging against God will turn their hearts to him. And what is the truth that everyone will confess?

> Wherefore God also hath highly exalted him, and given him a name which is above every name: That at the name

> of Jesus every knee should bow, of things in heaven, and things in earth, and things under the earth; And that every tongue should confess that Jesus Christ is Lord, to the glory of God the Father. (Philippians 2:9–11)

Again, every member of creation will ultimately arrive at the truth, and it will set them free.[9] All will confess that Jesus Christ is Lord, which cannot be done apart from the Holy Spirit.[10] This oath assures us they are now believers in Jesus Christ:[11]

> If anyone acknowledges that Jesus is the Son of God, God lives in them and they in God. (1 John 4:15 NIV)

God wants each of us to arrive at the truth on our own. If he had wanted robotic allegiance, he could have simply created us that way. Instead, we are free to choose. Once we have exhausted all other avenues of doing things our own way and we finally see the glorious truth of God's loving grace, every last one of us will find him waiting patiently with open arms.

The Bible assures us Jesus came to save all men, not to condemn them.[12] Jesus promised not to cast out anyone who turns to him.[13] And Jesus is the same yesterday, today, and forever.[14] Why, then, do some suggest that God might stop loving us the instant we die? That would mean he suddenly *doesn't* care to save all men; that he *does* cast out some of those who turn to him; and that his feelings for us *do* change—a violation of all three promises.

Since there has never been a time in which everyone believed Jesus is Lord, it is clear that the victorious culmination in which every knee bows and every tongue confesses must take place at some point in the future. This will only happen when every single member of creation confesses that Jesus is Lord "to the glory of God the Father."[15] It is impossible for this to occur if even *one single person* remains deceived, rebellious, or stuck in torment. Adoration is not achieved by force. This prophetic promise proves indisputably that at some future date, all anguish must end. Whatever punishments lie ahead for mankind cannot last forever.

When the word "all" appears in the Bible, it means *all*. But in a weak attempt to defend the flawed modern creed, proponents of endless torment insist that *all* really means *some*. Not only is this a shameful distortion, it is demonstrably false: a plain reading of other scriptures directly contradicts the notion that only *some* will be saved. Several verses repeatedly emphasize that God is the savior of *all* people, without making any distinctions:

> That is why we labor and strive, because we have put our hope in the living God, who is the Savior of *all* people, and especially of those who believe. (1 Timothy 4:10 NIV, *emphasis added*)

This verse is striking. In fact, it's difficult to imagine a sentence that could convey the point more forcefully: some of the saved are described as *believers*. Obviously, then, some of the saved are *not* believers. And regardless of who believes today, or whether they died before believing, there can be no question that God will be "the Savior of all people" just as this verse describes, since he has promised that at some point in the future *all* will confess that Jesus is Lord "to the glory of God the Father."

All people die. No one denies this. Yet many deny that the same *all* will be brought back to life in Christ, even though this point is made abundantly clear:

> For as in Adam *all* die, even so in Christ shall *all* be made alive. (1 Corinthians 15:22, *emphasis added*)

The Greek word rendered "all" twice in this verse is identical in both occurrences. Again, the full measure of the word in assuring *death* for all is undeniable, yet some are unwilling to apply it with equal force to *life* for all. It is unmistakable that the same group that dies—all—will also be given new life in Christ. To be certain, this is much more than mere reanimation for the sake of being tortured: the Greek word translated "be made alive" is derived from *zōopoieō*, which means not merely restored to life, but an

increase in life.[16] The nature and power of the abundant gift of
life is clear in this verse: we aren't made alive *by* Christ, but *in*
Christ. Eventually all will experience resurrection as he did.

What if you purchased airline tickets for your family, but were
given one less than you bought? One family member would be
left behind, even though you paid for everyone to go. Would you
be okay with this? Never! Likewise, Jesus paid the full price to
take away the sin of the world. He would never be satisfied if
the ransom he paid for *everyone* only freed half of mankind. This
would make Jesus' life worth less than he expected. God would
never be satisfied with losing one third of us, or one tenth, or even
one single person, because that is precisely why he sent Jesus here:
to take away the sins of the *whole* world.

What is the price that Jesus paid? Was he annihilated, and no
longer exists? No. Will he forever burn in flames of torment?
Certainly not.[17] The price paid is exactly what God promised; the
wages of sin is death.[18] *Death* is the consequence of sin. Though
sinless, Jesus took upon himself the iniquity of all mankind, and
was put to death—but he didn't stay dead. He demonstrated
power over death when he rose to incorruptible life. All will
inherit this same gift of life just as surely as we inherited death.

As Jesus said on the cross, it is finished. The price for all was
paid in full. Of course, not everyone realizes this yet. Salvation is
still being worked out in each person, each in his own order. Not
all men will receive the truth of Jesus' purpose in this lifetime.

The future appears to be quite different for those who believe
in Jesus now, as compared to those who do not. However, the
ultimate end result—freedom from bondage to sin and decay, and
God's absolute victory over death—has already been secured for
everyone through Jesus Christ's sacrifice:

> For as in Adam *all* die, even so in Christ shall *all* be
> made alive. But *every* man in his own order: Christ the
> firstfruits; afterward they that are Christ's at his coming.

> Then cometh the end, when he shall have delivered up the
> kingdom to God, even the Father; when he shall have put
> down *all* rule and *all* authority and power. For he must
> reign, till he hath put *all* enemies under his feet. The last
> enemy that shall be destroyed is death. (1 Corinthians
> 15:22–26, *emphasis added*)

No other rule, no other authority, no other power will remain
except Jesus. There can be no enemies left standing. Deception,
rebellion, sin, and death will no longer exist. And then, after
Christ's total victory is achieved, comes the glorious culmination:

> And when *all* things shall be subdued unto him, then shall
> the Son also himself be subject unto him that put all things
> under him, that God may be *all* in *all.* (1 Corinthians
> 15:28, *emphasis added*)

True and total victory. That is exactly what the Bible describes.
No room for rebellion, no space for sin, no power but God's. Not
only does this image resonate with the conscience of those created
in God's image, it is the only logical outcome—and the only one
compatible with a God of both love and justice.

Compare this to what it would look like if Jesus were to lose
some of us to the adversary. In his preface to the second edition
of *Christ Triumphant*, Thomas Allin sums up the dilemma of the
outcome predicted by today's mainstream Christians:

> And so the curtain falls on the great drama of creation
> and redemption, presenting such as picture as this—a
> baffled Saviour, a victorious Devil, a ruined creation,
> sin triumphant—and so to continue forever—a heaven
> wholly base, a hell wholly miserable. Strong as these
> words are, they are not strong enough, for the horrors
> and the contradictions of the popular creed alike defy
> description. And these horrors are taught, these contra-
> dictions are believed in the face of the plainest teaching
> of God's two revelations, His primary revelation to our
> moral sense, His written revelation in Holy Scripture.[19]

Like countless others before me, I was taught that the wicked will burn forever in flames of endless torment, experiencing the tortures of a perpetual dying state while they continue to curse and rebel against God. That position is untenable in light of the Scriptures. Sadly, the two things modern Christianity brazenly assures us will continue to exist forever—sin and death—are the same two that God explicitly promises to *destroy*. How incredibly awkward.

God's plain words affirm the still small voice whispering to the hearts of so many who have struggled with the bizarre notion of a god that would permit everlasting torment. God's promises are clear: Nothing short of total victory will satisfy him. Jesus will never give up. Death's days are numbered.

ALL IN ALL

God's plan includes everyone. The totality of his victory is plainly proclaimed throughout the Bible. God "will have all men to be saved, and to come unto the knowledge of the truth" (1 Timothy 2:3–4). Jesus' purpose was to carry out God's will on earth (John 4:34). Jesus was given authority over all people (John 17:2), and will not turn away anyone that comes to him (John 6:37).

Jesus is the only mediator between God and man, who "gave himself as a ransom for all" (1 Timothy 2:6). He is the sacrifice that atones not merely for the sins of believers, "but also for the sins of the whole world" (1 John 2:2). The Christ is "the savior of the world" (John 4:42), and he will not lose a single one of those that God has given him (John 18:9).

Just as Adam's offense has brought death to all men, "even so in Christ shall all be made alive." This will not take place all at once, "But every man in his own order" (1 Corinthians 15:22–23).

God says "all souls are mine" (Ezekiel 18:4). Upon death, "the spirit shall return unto God who gave it" (Ecclesiastes 12:7). The final "restitution of all things" will take place in the future, when every member of creation will be restored and returned to God, their rightful owner—a promise "which God hath spoken by the mouth of all his holy prophets since the world began" according to Acts 3:20–21.

God is working "to reconcile all things unto himself ... whether they be things in earth, or things in heaven" through Christ who "made peace through the blood of his cross" (Colossians 1:19–20). God is reconciling the world to himself through Jesus Christ, not counting their sins against them (2 Corinthians 5:18–19).

God will restore his relationship with mankind by removing the veil of blindness that prevents us from seeing the truth today (Isaiah 25:7). The glory of God will then be revealed to all men, "and all flesh shall see it together" (Isaiah 40:5).

One day God's creation "shall be delivered from the bondage of corruption" and freed at last (Romans 8:21). All creation will be made right, and "all people will see God's salvation" (Luke 3:5–6 NIV). We will be given incorruptible bodies (Philippians 3:20–21) of a different nature (1 Corinthians 15:44). This will require some to endure a second death (Revelation 20:14). Once it has served its purpose, God "will swallow up death in victory; and the Lord God will wipe away tears from off all faces" (Isaiah 25:8). There will be "no more death, neither sorrow, nor crying, neither shall there be any more pain," and the old order of things will no longer be (Revelation 21:4). Death will be the last enemy God destroys (1 Corinthians 15:26), resulting in life for all.

Despite rejecting Christ in this age, "all Israel shall be saved" because God "shall take away their sins" (Romans 11:25–32). God says, "I will forgive their iniquity, and I will remember their sin no more" (Jeremiah 31:33–34). Even Sodom and Samaria, the cities of unbelievers destroyed by God for their wickedness, will one day be restored (Ezekiel 16:55).

God has "made known to us the mystery of his will according to his good pleasure," which is to ultimately "bring unity to all things in heaven and on earth under Christ" (Ephesians 1:9–10 NIV). After he "has destroyed all dominion, authority and power," then Jesus himself will be subject to God the Father, "so that God may be all in all" (1 Corinthians 15:24–28).

All in all.

These three words depict the beautiful culmination of God's plan for mankind. The first instance of "all" represents God and his provision; the second is who receives it. God isn't satisfied with "some in all," or "all in some." He's going to fully and finally meet *all* needs for *all* people: God will *be* all *in* all.

This promised final state of creation—which includes everyone who ever lived—is clearly presented in 1 Corinthians chapter 15. If you think it's possible that God would leave even one single person out, take a moment to read this passage carefully and ask yourself: *What is God trying to tell us?* My hope is that your eyes will be opened, and you will begin to grasp the absolute finality and limitless reach of a victory befitting the sovereign God of the universe. He will share us with no one else.

What God has purposed will stand (Isaiah 14:24–27), and he will do everything he pleases: "I have spoken it, I will also bring it to pass; I have purposed it, I will also do it" (Isaiah 46:10–11). God is in complete control. He is patiently waiting on each of us to turn to him (Revelation 3:20). And he has all the time, power and patience in the world with which to bring it about.

He will settle for nothing less.

CHAPTER 14

HISTORY

*That men do not learn very much
from the lessons of history is the most important
of all the lessons that history has to teach.*

— ALDOUS HUXLEY

U PON LEARNING that the Bible foretells the reconciliation of all creation, some may wonder why they haven't heard of this before. After all, if this is really the gospel message God wants to convey to his creation, why aren't most churches teaching it?

As we've seen, many passages clearly promise Christ's ultimate victory over sin and death, and the resurrection and restoration of all mankind. Despite this, we must acknowledge that most church leaders are hesitant to depart from the doctrine of endless torment they were trained to teach. Because of this, it is important to consider evidence of what the very first followers of Christ taught, rather than focusing solely on modern religious trends.

Paul is certainly the earliest church father to consider. In his many letters to fledgling churches, he reiterated and clarified the core beliefs for early followers of Jesus. Some of the clearest verses that address the reconciliation of all people were penned by Paul. A plain reading of his original writings—or a reliable translation—leaves no doubt that Paul's concept of salvation was unlimited in both scope and power.

However, it would help to have notes and writings *outside* of the Bible to determine what the earliest church fathers taught. Did they believe all people would ultimately be saved? Or did they instead promote endless torment, as today's most prominent evangelical Christian leaders do?

EARLY PATRISTIC WRITINGS

CLEMENT OF ALEXANDRIA (C. AD 150–215)

First, let's consider one of the earliest teachers. Near the end of the second century, Clement of Alexandria (also known as Titus Flavius Clemens) observed:

> And how is He Saviour and Lord, if not the Saviour and Lord of all? But He is the Saviour of those who have believed, because of their wishing to know; and the Lord of those who have not believed, till, being enabled to confess him, they obtain the peculiar and appropriate boon which comes by Him.[1]

Based on his writings, which were among the earliest penned after Christ's resurrection, there is no doubt Clement believed *all* men would ultimately be saved. In a commentary on 1 John 2:2, he writes:

> "And not only for our sins,"—that is for those of the faithful,—is the Lord the propitiator, does he say, "but also for the whole world." He, indeed, saves all; but some [He saves], converting them by punishments; others, however, who follow voluntarily [He saves] with dignity of honour; so "that every knee should bow to Him, of things in heaven, and things on earth, and things under the earth;" that is, angels, men, and souls that before His advent have departed from this temporal life.[2]

Clearly, Clement didn't just teach that all *men* would be saved: he taught that *all* of God's creatures would eventually be reconciled to God through Jesus, including angels.

ORIGEN (C. AD 184–253)

Clement's belief in the ultimate reconciliation of all is a radical departure from today's mainstream Christianity. Was he alone in his understanding? Far from it. Origen of Alexandria (Origen Adamantius) was one of the most influential early church fathers. As a very prolific church writer, he is among the most notable Christian theologians that ever lived. He taught that

> An end or consummation would seem to be an indication of the perfection and completion of things. ... The end of the world, then, and the final consummation, will take place when every one shall be subjected to punishment for his sins; a time which God alone knows, when He will bestow on each one what he deserves. We think, indeed, that the goodness of God, through His Christ, may recall all His creatures to one end, even His enemies being conquered and subdued.[3]

In a separate work, he describes God's plan to heal and perfect every member of creation to attain this final state:

> But our belief is, that the Word shall prevail over the entire rational creation, and change every soul into His own perfection ... For stronger than all the evils in the soul is the Word, and the healing power that dwells in Him; and this healing He applies, according to the will of God, to every man. ... Many things are said obscurely in the prophecies on the total destruction of evil, and the restoration to righteousness of every soul...[4]

Of course, early theologians differed on many things, but belief in the reconciliation of all was common. In the early years of the Christian church, writings like these were by no means unusual, and went largely unopposed. What *was* considered unorthodox were heathen and Gnostic views that denied God's benevolence, and Origen often argued against these.[5] Sadly, the heresies he once fought are now so prevalent that if they were alive today, the earliest church fathers would be ridiculed by modern popular Christian lay-leaders.

TITUS OF BOSTRA (DIED C. AD 371)

Titus of Bostra, a fourth-century Christian theologian, agreed that any future punishment endured by God's creatures would not be permanent, but rather temporary and curative:

> [The] abyss of hell is, indeed, the place of torment; but it is not eternal, nor did it exist in the original constitution of nature. It was made afterwards, as a remedy for sinners, that it might cure them. And the punishments are holy, as they are remedial and salutary in their effect upon transgressors; for they are inflicted, not to preserve them in their wickedness, but to make them cease from their wickedness.[6]

Like many other early teachers, Titus held that God's discipline had a *corrective* aim, rather than simply to torture. They taught that the goal of punishment was to ultimately bring about the final reconciliation of all creatures to God.

GREGORY NYSSEN (C. AD 335–395)

Commenting on chapter 15 of Paul's first letter to the Corinthians, Gregory of Nyssa provides a clear description of the ultimate extermination of all evil:

> What, therefore, is the scope of St. Paul's dissertation in this place? That the nature of evil shall, at length, be wholly exterminated, and divine, immortal goodness embrace within itself every rational creature; so that of all who were made by God, not one shall be excluded from his kingdom. All the viciousness, that like a corrupt

matter is mingled in things, shall be dissolved and consumed in the furnace of purgatorial fire; and every thing that had its origin from God, shall be restored to its pristine state of purity.[7]

Phrases like "all who were made by God" make it very clear that Gregory has *all* creatures in view—not merely followers of Christ in this life. In fact, he asserts that Satan

assumed a fleshly shape in order to ruin human nature, so the Lord took flesh for the salvation of man; and thus he blesses not only him who was ruined, but him also who led him into perdition so that he both delivers man from sin, and heals the author of sin himself.[8]

Since he taught that *Satan himself* was to be delivered, there is no doubt Gregory believed every last *person* would ultimately be saved too. No matter how wicked, and no matter whether they died an unbeliever, nobody would miss out.

BELIEVED BY MANY

The ultimate reconciliation of all was undeniably familiar to and taught by the earliest Christian teachers, and was likely the most commonly held view.[9] Several ancient records confirm its wide prevalence among the first followers of Jesus. For example, Saint Basil the Great recognized that

The mass of men say that there is to be an end of punishment to those who are punished.[10]

Similarly, Saint Jerome observed that most people believed all creatures would ultimately be forgiven, including Satan:

I know that most persons understand the story of Nineveh and its king, the ultimate forgiveness of the devil and all rational creatures.[11]

Even Augustine of Hippo, who would champion endless torment and become one of the strongest influences on modern Western theology, admitted that the majority disagreed with his view:

> There are very many in our day, who though not denying the Holy Scriptures, do not believe in endless torments.[12]

SHIFTING ORTHODOX VIEWS

There was very little controversy about the restitution of all things among Christians for at least three centuries after the death of Christ.[13, 14, 15] The modern doctrine of endless torture developed much later, under the influence of pagan traditions, championed by men unfamiliar with the Bible's original languages.[16]

Several hundred years into the church's existence, the teaching that some would be subjected to endless punishment began to gain traction, but remained in the minority. Six principal schools of theology existed in the centuries following Origen, and four of them taught the restoration of all. Only two did not:

> Of these six schools, one, and only one, was decidedly and earnestly in favor of the doctrine of future eternal punishment. One was in favor of the annihilation of the wicked.[17]

Unfortunately, the opposite is now true: the restitution of all promised by God appears to be largely uncertain, unknown, or unwelcome. For the last thousand years, influential Christian leaders have banished unbelievers to everlasting torment with an incredibly brazen air of certainty.

Given the widespread early belief in the salvation of all, it comes as no surprise that the first ecumenical councils expressed no opposition to it: the First Council of Nicaea in AD 325, the First Council of Constantinople, the Council of Ephesus, and the Council of Chalcedon did not denounce the ultimate reconciliation of all—nor did they endorse endless torment. And it wasn't until AD 553, over five and a half centuries into the church's existence, that the Fifth Ecumenical Council was said to have first condemned a doctrine related to the salvation of all.

In light of the historical record, today's thoughtful Christian is certainly in line with the earliest followers of Christ to believe that all people will ultimately be saved, and to pray for the salvation of every person.[18]

LATER INFLUENCES

Of course, not everyone taught Christ would emerge victorious. Augustine of Hippo (c. 354–430) was gaining prominence as an influential theologian. A strong advocate for endless torment, his writings would fundamentally shape modern Christianity. He taught that one's afterlife—whether they were sent to heaven or hell—was sealed for eternity based on whether they had placed their faith in Jesus before dying.

However, we should carefully note two key points regarding Augustine's background. First, before converting to Christianity, Augustine was a follower of Manichaeism, a Persian religion founded in the third century that describes a conflict between two eternal powers of good and evil. Tellingly, the tenets of this Gnostic belief system are virtually identical to the new picture Augustine began to paint for later Christians: God—who is good, but not quite omnipotent—is eternally at odds with a powerful force of evil (Satan) in a conflict that never quite gets resolved. This is unquestionably a form of *dualism*.

Second—and equally unnerving—is the fact that Augustine had an admittedly weak grasp of the Greek language, and little to no understanding of Hebrew. This is profoundly significant: the Septuagint on which he primarily relied was written in Greek. Since this was the native language of the earliest church fathers, they were far more capable of discerning the precise meanings of the original text. Augustine was not. Accordingly, Augustine should not be regarded as a preeminent authority where his interpretations are at odds with those who had mastery of the original languages.

Despite these grave concerns, his teachings gained popularity and were closely followed by Martin Luther, John Calvin, and many others, heavily influencing the Protestant Reformation and modern Christian theology. This eventually paved the way for today's Christian dualism: an endless conflict between God and Satan in which sin and death are never destroyed.

Either Augustine was right... or Jesus is the Savior of *all*.

CHAPTER 15

LOVE

Anyone who does not love does not know God,
because God is love.

— 1 JOHN 4:8

THE MORNING after our first child was born, I was sitting in a chair in the hospital, awkwardly cradling her in my new-daddy arms. My wife had briefly left the two of us alone in the room. In all the excitement, reality hadn't completely set in yet. I began to feel the gravity of that wonderful occasion. Such a blessing, coupled with such enormous responsibility.

My eyes welled up with tears of joy looking down at this tiny little face. She was completely helpless. In the coming years, she would rely on us for every need, every comfort... everything. The very words she would express herself with would be learned from us. Her concepts of family and love and happiness would come directly from what she would see inside our home. And in that special moment we shared, I promised that her mother and I would always take care of her, always be there for her, always love her. *Nothing you can do will change that,* I whispered. *There is absolutely nothing you can ever do to lose my love. Nothing.*

Now, years later, we tell our children every day that we love them, and that there is nothing they can ever do to change that. Maybe you can relate to this. Maybe not. Not all of us have had the chance to know our parents, or to receive the kind of love we had hoped for—but we all know the kind of love we want.

In practice, our concept of love is quite lacking. Our minds are often marred by a *quid pro quo* concept of love. In giving, we usually expect to receive. This approach to life treats each inter-action—even our closest relationships—as a contract, transaction, or purchase. Almost all we have to offer is conditional: *I will agree to do that,* we stipulate, *as long as you will do this.*

True love is a difficult thing to give. It can even be hard to recognize and accept when it is offered to us. Few know what real love is, and even fewer are capable of giving it—yet everyone wants it. We long for the safety of complete acceptance.

Unconditional love is what we seek from our parents. Care and encouragement from our parents form an irreplaceable bond. I find it interesting that God arranged for our lives to begin completely dependent upon others. It could have been very different: Humans could have sprouted from vines instead. Once ripe, they would fall to the ground, fairly self-sufficient, able to walk and talk with a little practice. We'd show the new ones around, teach them the basics, then turn them loose. But it's nothing like this. It's far more difficult. Instead of spawning or hatching as mature adults, we are birthed as helpless infants. Everything we need to survive must be provided by our parents, and all we know—how to act, eat, talk, love—will be learned from them. The child is fully reliant, the parent fully responsible.

By design, every single person participates in some form of a parent-child relationship. This provides insight into God's deep desire to relate to us. Whether a caretaker's love is ideal or sorely lacking, we are given the opportunity to learn what love is—or perhaps what it is not. Even when parents fail miserably, their shortcomings shape our concept of what love *should* have been, which allows us to improve upon it for the sake of our own relationships. Parent-child interactions give us the ability to see how God relates to us: the love he has for us, our helpless reliance on him, and his responsibility to look after every one of those he brought into existence.

We inherit the image of our parents, and we look and act like them. You and I were created in God's image. God is responsible for creating us. Like an infant, we rely on him for every single breath. But does God love like we do? Might he feel the same way a human father does when he cradles his helpless child in his arms, and promises to love her no matter what?

God doesn't love like we do... No, his love is *far* better. There are three huge differences between regular parents and God. First, God's love is much greater because it is endless and unconditional. Second, God is more powerful. Unlike regular parents, he is able to fully and permanently fix anything that ails his children. Third, God is the ultimate father of creation. We can't create children from nothing, but God did—he chose to create us for his own pleasure—and he wants us to rely on him for everything.

TRUE LOVE

We love our kids. We love sports. We love hot dogs. We rarely say, "I'm extremely fond of mustard." No, we *love* mustard. (Unless we *hate* it!) Clearly the word "love" can describe a wide spectrum of feelings. Maybe we tend to overuse it a little.

There are a few different Greek words available to accurately describe relationships and various types of affection. However, these unique original words are almost always translated to "love" in English, and important distinctions may be lost. What a shame. The unfortunate result is that our modern English translations may convey seemingly equal force to Jesus Christ's love for mankind as we might express for donuts.

When "love" appears in an English translation of a Greek text, the original word is commonly *eros, philia,* or *agape.* The first, *eros,* reflects a passion that is physical or sensual in nature—a feeling of chemistry or love at first sight. *Philia* is a love for family or friends: love seated in the mind. And *agape* is a selfless love, given freely without regard for what is given in return. Since it is completely unconditional, it may also translate to "charity."

It is not uncommon to hear 1 Corinthians chapter 13 read aloud at a Christian wedding ceremony. This passage contains God's definition of true, unconditional *agape* love:

> Love is patient, love is kind. It does not envy, it does not boast, it is not proud. It does not dishonor others, it is not self-seeking, it is not easily angered, it keeps no record of wrongs. Love does not delight in evil but rejoices with the truth. It always protects, always trusts, always hopes, always perseveres. Love never fails.[1]

Not many people have received true love, yet this is exactly what every child, parent, spouse—every *person*—longs to feel. It is hard to love others in this way. How do we react when it isn't reciprocated? When we are taken for granted? Disrespected? Once the object of our affection hurts us and the limits of our love are tested, conditions of the arrangement become evident.

In 1 John 4:8 and 16 we are assured that "God is love." What a declaration! Now, if God were simply the type of contractual love we're so accustomed to, this is no great revelation—but here we are given the definition of *agape.* And since God *is* love, we can read his definition of it in the passage above from 1 Corinthians 13:4–8, and replace each instance of "love" with "God." Take a moment to try it... you just might see God in a new light.

God didn't merely love us first: he *is* love. It is manifested in the person and sacrifice of Jesus Christ. His desire is for us to love as he does. When asked which is the greatest commandment of all, Jesus said we should first love God with all our heart, soul, and mind; and second, we should love our neighbor as ourself. These two commandments are the entire premise of God's revelations to mankind.[2] Love is the greatest gift of all.[3]

FATHER OF CREATION

God tells us the souls of every father and son belong to him.[4] While this invokes the familiar parent-child relationship, it also reveals that we are all peers, regardless of our present roles in relation to one another.

Our focus is typically on the hierarchy of our relationships. We picture a family tree in which we fit between our parents and our children, and rarely look past these roles. This may obscure the fact that all men are equal in the eyes of God. In reality, parents are just people who came into existence a couple of decades before their children. A short span of time is all that distinguishes us. Of course, parents must take care of their children, and children must obey their parents. These are the temporal duties inherent in each role. But one day both the parent and the child will stand as equals before God, without regard for who was born first.

When each person dies, our spirit returns to the creator who gave us life.[5] God alone brought us into existence, and we were formed in his image.[6] We breathe because his life-giving spirit animates us. Mankind belongs to God, the ultimate father of all creation.[7] God requires parents to care for their children because it is their responsibility.[8] Likewise, we are God's creation and his responsibility, and he is looking after us as a loving father would. Luckily for us, God's love is far superior.

ILLUSTRATIONS OF GOD'S LOVE

Insight into God's love can be gleaned from various relationships we take part in. Consider the animal kingdom entrusted to us. We are expected to be good stewards of God's creation, and to provide compassionate care for helpless creatures.

Sheep, for example, must be tended to, looked after, and guarded with great care because they are ignorant of the dangers around them. Compared to the infinite wisdom of God, we are a lot like sheep. We don't understand all that is going on in the world around us. We're mostly caught up in the moment. God looks after us like a devoted shepherd, even though we may not realize we need his help.

In Luke chapter 15, Jesus uses a series of parables to illustrate God's loving resolve to rescue every last one of us. In the first, a lost sheep has wandered away from the others, and can't find its way back. The loving shepherd leaves his flock of ninety-nine sheep to search for the one that has gone astray until he finds it. When he finally does, he doesn't scold or punish it:

> And when he finds it, he joyfully puts it on his shoulders and goes home. Then he calls his friends and neighbors together and says, "Rejoice with me; I have found my lost sheep." I tell you that in the same way there will be more rejoicing in heaven over one sinner who repents than over ninety-nine righteous persons who do not need to repent. (Luke 15:5–7 NIV)

God is passionately pursuing those who don't yet know him. We may continue to put distance between ourselves and God, but the Good Shepherd has already initiated the search himself, and he will persist until every single one of his creatures is saved.

The second parable tells of a woman who loses one of her ten pieces of silver. Unable to rest, she lights a candle, sweeps the house, and searches until she finds it. Once it is found, she rejoices with her friends. But the choice of a coin in this analogy is telling, since a coin can neither lose nor find itself. The actions of the lost item are of no consequence; rather, it is the owner that is credited with its recovery through relentless pursuit. God, the rightful owner of all people, will continue his search until all are found. *His* faithfulness—not ours—is what saves us.

The third parable describes a young man who decides to leave home, and asks his father for his inheritance early. Reluctantly, his father agrees. The young man goes on to squander his wealth. Shortly thereafter, he is working in a field feeding pigs when he realizes he has made a mess of things. He then returns home to ask his father for forgiveness, pleading for a job as a servant. The father, rather than being angry, rejoices and prepares a great feast to celebrate his prodigal son's return.

God is clearly not okay with losing anyone. Jesus used each of these illustrations to express how valuable each one of us is to God, and to assure us that he will never stop seeking us. Just like the sheep, the coin, and the foolish son, mankind is operating at an enormous disadvantage in that we know far less about what is going on than our rightful owner does. If God were to give up, we would all lose—especially him.

FULL OF MERCY

Jesus was beaten and tortured hours before his crucifixion. As he hung from the cross before his taunting executioners, his bones were likely slipping out of joint. Despite this humiliating demise, Jesus did not consume them with a pillar of fire, but had great mercy. As his murderers watched him die, Jesus pleaded with God, "Father, forgive them; for they know not what they do."[9]

It is extremely difficult to imagine a more powerful image of love in action. Here is the Christ, the sacrifice who came to take away the sin of the world, being slain at the hands of those he came to help. Even as we spit upon him, mocked him, and took his life away, he remained steadfastly focused on helping his beloved creation. Can we do anything to lose the love of Jesus?

There is absolutely nothing you can ever do to lose my love.

Some paint God the Father as full of anger—ready to strike us down at any moment, were it not for Jesus the loving mediator. This is incorrect. Jesus *is* God. God came to us as Jesus. Jesus came to do God's will. God didn't send his Son to condemn man, but to save him.[10] God did this because he *loved* the world—*agape* love—in a way that perseveres, keeps no record of wrongs, and never fails. God loves each of us unconditionally.

Man, who longs to be loved, thirsts for God. God *is* love, and he designed us in his image with a void only he can fill. Meanwhile, we struggle to find purpose or pleasure in food, religion, sex, drugs, shopping, music, sports, or any other mind-numbing distraction—but nothing will ever replace the innate need for true love from our creator.

It is love that moved God to create us. To show us the difference between good and evil. To send his Son to die on the cross. It is the same love that made Christ plead for our forgiveness as we murdered him. This is the source of God's limitless compassion. His mercy endures forever.[11]

This weekend, many churches will sing songs of praise that emphasize God's unending love and mercy—only to preach a message afterward that denies his promises, and insists that God's patience and grace end the moment an unbeliever dies. Many who love God with all their heart still do not know his.

> Dear friends, let us love one another, for love comes from God. Everyone who loves has been born of God and knows God. Whoever does not love does not know God, because God is love. (1 John 4:7–8 NIV)

God promises us that his mercy endures forever, he never gives up, and he never changes. He promises that one day every knee will bow and every tongue confess that Jesus is Lord to the glory of God. He promises to reject no one. He promises to completely destroy sin and death. He even came to tell stories about how he will never be satisfied until every last one of us has been reconciled to him. He even assures us, "I am making everything new!"[12]

Do you believe him?

CHAPTER 16

GRACE

To be convinced in our hearts that we have forgiveness of
sins and peace with God by grace alone is the hardest thing.

— Martin Luther

"B ust him, Bone!" shouted an older gang member one evening
in San Diego, California in 1995. "Bone" was Tony Hicks,
a troubled 14-year-old child living with his grandfather. Tony
pulled the trigger, shooting 20-year-old Tariq Khamisa, a student
working part time to supplement his income by delivering pizzas.
It was Tariq's last delivery for the evening, and the last moments
of his life.

As part of a gang initiation, Tony was to steal a pizza without
paying for it. When Tariq refused to turn it over, the youth was
instructed to shoot him. The life of a bright young student ended
abruptly that night for a pizza. Tony became the first 14-year-old
to stand trial as an adult in the state of California. He entered a
guilty plea and was sentenced to a 25-year prison term.

If you were the victim's father, could you forgive his cold-
blooded killer? Most could not. It seems unthinkable, yet this is
what Tariq's father, Azim, did. He forgave Tony for murdering

his son over a pizza, and wrote a letter to the governor requesting Tony's sentence be commuted to reduce his punishment.

Could you show the same grace to your child's murderer? Would you make an effort to befriend him? Petition for his early release from prison? Would you view the tragedy as the loss of *two* lives, rather than just one? It's hard to imagine, but this is what true forgiveness looks like. We don't see it often.

Azim remained focused on forgiveness rather than anger. He established a foundation in his son's name in an effort to stop the cycle of violence among children. Azim paired up with Tony's grandfather, traveling and speaking throughout the country to promote a moving message of peace and forgiveness. Together they reflect on the senseless tragedy of violence that struck both families, resulting in Tariq's death and Tony's incarceration.

Five years into Tony's sentence, Azim visited him in prison and described it as "a very healing time." He told Tony that as soon as he was released from prison, he would have a job waiting at the foundation. Afterward, Tony said to his grandfather, "That is a very special man. I shot and killed his one and only son and yet he can sit with me, encourage me, and then offer me a job."[1]

When a criminal is pardoned of an offense, it's as though the crime never happened. It is complete forgiveness. Although Tony continues to serve his sentence for the state, he has been pardoned by the one his actions hurt most: the victim's father. Azim wakes up every day without his only son, yet he forgives. His grace has had a profound impact on Tony and others who learn their story.

True forgiveness seems rare and baffling—almost unnatural. When it is extended to us we might feel like hidden conditions are attached, even when they aren't. And when it's our turn to forgive, it can often seem impossible to pardon those who have wounded us deeply. As with true love, mankind can barely grasp the concept of true grace. Like Azim, those who forgive often cite their faith as a source of strength, which is unsurprising: forgiveness goes against our learned selfish inclinations. It reflects a rare spiritual ability to look past current circumstances and see every member of mankind through the eyes of the Creator, in which all have value and all are loved. This understanding awakens and is awakened by our original design in God's image.

Perhaps grace is intriguing and deeply moving because it is a gift that can't be earned. Grace can only be given.

A FOREIGN CONCEPT

The Code of Hammurabi is a set of ancient Babylonian laws found inscribed on a stone pillar dated circa 1770 BC. It is the source of the phrase "an eye for an eye." The concept seems quite brutal, and it is. But it actually served to *reduce* brutality by ensuring that retribution did not exceed the original crime. It prevented extreme vengeance: a man who lost one eye at the hands of his enemy would not be allowed to gouge *both* of the violator's eyes out for punishment... just one.

Society has since progressed toward more civilized norms. For example, if a negligent driver strikes a pedestrian, the victim isn't given a chance to drive over the perpetrator to settle the score. Relief is limited to criminal and civil judgments in a court of law. In ancient times, however, exacting physical justice was the law of the land, as mentioned in the Old Testament.[2] But Jesus taught his followers a higher code of forgiveness: when struck, they were to turn the other cheek. In the sermon on the mount recorded in Matthew chapter 5, Jesus exhorts us to love our enemies, bless those that curse us, do good to those that hate us, and pray for those who use or persecute us. He also teaches that if someone sues us for our coat, we are to give them our cloak as well.

These rules are very hard to live by, but total forgiveness is what Jesus expects. He didn't tell his followers to be nice to their friendly neighbors—he commanded them to love their *enemies*. A follower of Christ is to forgive all, just as they have been forgiven.

Jesus wouldn't instruct us to forgive our enemies if he himself weren't willing to do the same. God provided the perfect sacrifice to forgive all sins, including murdering his only son. This is the grace extended to us, which we must extend to others. We are not to merely *offer* forgiveness; we are to completely forgive.

GRACE IS GREATER

Destruction works against itself. It is self-limiting. If a disease were to kill every living thing, it would no longer present a threat since it would have eradicated the very life it depends on.

Sin works the same way. Thieves and liars work to undermine and destroy each other to get ahead. In the end, each is brought down by the consequences of their own behavior. Those who commit heinous crimes often carry a burden of guilt that leads to denial, depression, and death. Sin is effectively killing itself off by destroying its hosts.

Grace is the exact opposite. Its viral impact brings life and inspiration, unlimited in scope. It transcends an existence focused solely on self. Grace celebrates life and allows us to see a bigger picture. It gives hope, evokes love, and sets us free. Grace heals.

Adam's choice to defy God allowed death to enter the human race, and through death, sin now afflicts all mankind. His single act of disobedience resulted in condemnation for everyone.

That's the bad news.

The good news is that Jesus' single act of righteousness—his sacrifice on the cross—is to bring "justification and life for all people."[3] The original Greek word for *justification* refers to the act of God declaring men free from guilt.[4] But how does this work?

The Bible refers to Jesus as "the last Adam."[5] This analogy shows how Jesus' action on the cross and Adam's action in the garden both affect all mankind. Both began life sinless. Both were tempted by the adversary: Adam in the garden, Christ on the mountaintop. The first Adam gave in and made a selfish, poor choice. But Jesus, the last Adam, resisted—and he made a selfless, righteous choice.

As individuals, we did not participate in either of these choices, yet each impacts all members of humanity with equal force.[6] Adam didn't consult with you before making his decision, and you didn't participate in his actions. Regardless, everyone has been hurt by his choice and will certainly die as a result. Neither did you contribute to Jesus' act of righteousness. Regardless, everyone will be blessed by it: all will rise to life again through the justification Christ's sacrifice brings.[7]

To visualize what took place, imagine mankind's family tree, with Adam situated at the top. Every human that has ever lived is a descendant of this man. Adam held the seed of the entire human race inside his body before he fathered a single child. All of us were literally *in* Adam. So when Adam made his poor choice, all people inherited the consequences, just as it is written: "as in Adam, all die."

Where is Jesus in this family tree? While it is true that his lineage can be traced through Abraham and King David, this is a narrow view. In reality, Jesus is at the top, directly above Adam:

> He is the image of the invisible God, the firstborn of all creation. For by him all things were created ... all things were created through him and for him. And he is before all things, and in him all things hold together.[8]

In other words, before Adam generated all of humanity in his own image, Jesus first created Adam in *his.* Just as all Adam's descendants were in him, Adam and everyone else was originally in *Christ.* The family tree we envision often starts with Adam at the top, instead of placing Jesus in his rightful position as "the firstborn of all creation." A father's choice affects all his children. Both Adam and Christ, the "last Adam," made choices that impact all their descendants, regardless of their understanding. Just as Adam's choice *afflicted* all, Jesus' sacrifice will *heal* all. With the proper family tree in view, we begin to see how "as in Adam all die, so also in Christ shall all be made alive." Again, we're made alive not merely *by* Christ—as if from a distance—but *in* Christ, just as all were *in* Adam. In both cases we all inherit the result.

But there is a big difference. The blot of Adam's sin will pale in comparison to the power of the free gift of grace from Christ:

> But the free gift is not like the trespass. For if many died through one man's trespass, much more have the grace of God and the free gift by the grace of that one man Jesus Christ abounded for many. ... Therefore, as one trespass led to condemnation for all men, so one act of righteousness leads to justification and life for all men. (Romans 5:15, 18 ESV)

Once all are justified and brought back to incorruptible life, our bodies will be forever cured of the sin and death that ail us.[9] Death, and dying, will cease. Adam's sin brought death to all, but Christ's free gift of grace brings justification and life for all.

The question is simple: *Who is more powerful?* If we deny that Christ's choice brings life for *all*, then we must admit that Adam had a stronger impact on the human race than Jesus Christ.

SAVING GRACE

God's son sacrificed himself to free his creation from bondage to sin.[10] But it's important to recognize that merely reading and understanding this doesn't make one a follower of Jesus.

Atheists and agnostics understand the tenets of the Christian faith, and reject them. Evil spirits, on the other hand, "believe and shudder"—aware that Jesus is Lord—yet are evidently unwilling or unable to submit to Jesus at this time.[11] The adversary also knows exactly what is unfolding, and that time is running out.[12] Salvation clearly isn't obtained by learning a list of facts. Rather, it begins the moment we rely entirely on Jesus to provide it. This gift is permanent and can never be lost.[13] It is not faith in ourselves, or our choice to believe, or our good actions: it is faith alone in Christ alone. He does it all. We contribute nothing.

> If you declare with your mouth, "Jesus is Lord," and believe in your heart that God raised him from the dead, you will be saved. (Romans 10:9 NIV)

As promised, the time is coming when *every single tongue* will confess this truth, bringing glory to God the Father. Some of us already believe it now.[14] The rest will embrace it later. Because we aren't face to face with God, an element of faith is required at present. But in the future, faith and hope will no longer be necessary.[15] Once the truth is unveiled and seen by all, it will be believed and confessed by all—and all will be set free.

Faith in Jesus doesn't immediately solve the problems we face today. For example, we will still face death, since everyone must die at least once.[16] The moment we believe, the Holy Spirit indwells the heart and begins a spiritual awakening to provide peace, understanding, and strength. But the body still remains corrupted by sin until we are fully perfected, so the stings of pain, addiction, decay, mental illness, and disease persist in this life. Our salvation culminates when God cures us of sin and death by making us new, with an incorruptible and glorious body like Christ's.[17] The goal of becoming like Christ begins in this life, but is completed later. It is a struggle that ends in victory not because of our faith, but because of God's faithfulness.

A parent looks upon his child and is filled with joy at every milestone. Gurgling word-like noises, clumsy first steps, and botched handwriting are celebrated not because they are grand achievements, but in anticipation for the future: the father is full of joy and hope. He wants his children to stand upon his shoulders, to outperform him, and to be a blessing to the world. When God looks at us, he is also filled with joy... but not hope. For God, a bright future hinges not on wishful thinking, but on the certainty that he himself will bring it about. *God's* achievements deliver the grand final result, not ours. We are merely beneficiaries.

Jesus' sacrifice on the cross gave the free gift of grace to all mankind. All have sinned, yet God sent himself to pardon us all, no matter what lies in our past. Some Christians have derided this as "cheap grace." They say this makes it too easy; that a follower of Jesus must also do good works or make good choices to be saved. But the term "cheap grace" is inherently silly. Like "hot ice," it is an oxymoron. It can be cheap or it can be grace, but it can't be both. Placing a price on grace—such as good deeds—makes it a conditional transaction rather than a free gift. But grace, by definition, is completely free: it is *unmerited favor*.[18]

God's grace isn't "cheap." It's breathtaking. And it cost him the ultimate price: his only son. There is no greater love than "to lay down one's life for one's friends" (John 15:13).

EACH IN HIS OWN ORDER

Once he sets his sights on us, we are hopelessly drawn to God's loving grace. Nothing can stop his love from taking hold of us. We cannot turn away from the one who designed us in his own likeness, and neither can he turn away and abandon his beloved creation, the object of his unending love.

Seeing the truth makes the offer of grace irresistible. Chapter 9 of Acts describes the conversion of a man that illustrates how quickly a heart turns to God once our eyes are opened. Saul was a Jew from Tarsus who had never met Jesus, but rejected him as a false messiah. After Jesus' death, Saul worked to persecute and destroy the early Christian church. He hated Christians.

He was definitely *not* interested in following Jesus.

Then one day, as Saul was traveling with a group of men on the road to Damascus to capture more Christians and deliver them up for punishment, he was blinded by a bright light. The other men around him heard a voice, but could see no one. "Saul, Saul, why do you persecute me?" asked the voice. "I am Jesus, whom you persecute."[19] This brief encounter resulted in a dramatic conversion: Saul would later become known as Paul the Apostle, preach that Jesus was the Christ, write many of the letters found in the New Testament, be imprisoned for his faith, and die a martyr.

This change confounded many, given Saul's anti-Christian past. He was headed the wrong way entirely when Jesus intervened. He didn't seek it, didn't pray for it, and didn't deserve it—but when Christ called his name, he was immediately changed. Once the veil of misunderstanding was pulled aside and the scales had fallen from his eyes, he discovered the truth of God's gracious gift of salvation for all. Without God's help, Saul never would have confessed Jesus is Lord.[20]

If God can do this for Saul, he can do it for anyone. *Everyone.*

Jesus came to take away the sins of the world. Any subsequent faith we decide to place in him is the result of God's grace. Not only did God provide the perfect sacrifice to redeem all creation, but he also reveals the truth and provides the faith necessary to call upon him as our savior. Faith itself is given by God.[21]

Christ's sacrifice was a free gift. Salvation is a free gift. Even our faith is a free gift. Our decision to believe is the inevitable response to God's work. We believe and confess the truth because of the grace he has shown us. God takes care of every aspect of salvation so that no man can boast or take credit for it.[22]

Some emphasize the decision to believe as the key to salvation. They seem to believe Jesus did 99% of the work, but that their choice to believe constitutes the remaining 1% required to secure salvation—thus their choice makes all the difference, as it is what effectively saves them. But relying on others isn't taking action. Infants aren't credited with "choosing" to rely on their parents. It is a parent's responsibility to care for them. In reality, salvation is the result of faith given freely by God. We cannot have faith in Jesus apart from God's calling.[23] He does it all from start to finish.[24] Like an infant, the believer is incapable of contributing. We add *nothing*. And by relying on the works of a victorious and loving Father, rather than our own deeds, we are freed from a life of fear and uncertainty.[25]

Not every realization will be like Saul's. Still, no matter how or when he chooses to present the truth, God promises that his gifts and calling are irrevocable.[26] Once God decides the time is right, no rational creature can possibly refuse his offer. Once the veil is removed, we will always embrace God's love—freely, by our own choice—because it is the natural response for every creature made in God's image. He is all we were designed to long for. Each person will be saved in their own order, according to God's divine timeline.[27] Christ's total victory over sin and death cannot be thwarted by anyone.

Sodom was destroyed by God for its wickedness.[28] It will be restored at some point in the future.[29] But Jesus said that if he had performed his miracles in Sodom, they would have been spared.[30] That is a remarkable statement: If Jesus had revealed himself to them, just like he did for the anti-Christian Saul, they would have been saved? If it's that easy, why not do it for everyone?

And he will. Anything less would be unjust. It would amount to picking winners and losers. Eventually Jesus will reveal himself to all—including those who died rejecting him—after which they will call on him and be saved. No one has faith apart from God's intervention, and no one is beyond his reach. God will not rest until every last person calls upon his son Jesus Christ.

If you feel that God is unveiling the truth for you, please take a moment to read Romans 10:8–13.

CHAPTER 17

FREEDOM

He who has overcome his fears will truly be free.

— ARISTOTLE

G OD HAS the power to reveal the truth of Christ's sacrifice to us as he pleases. When he does, we believe, rely on him, and are saved. The simplicity of God's plan is beautiful.

Each person is free to call on Christ at any time, and all who do will be saved.[1] The question is not *whether* everyone will arrive at this same conclusion, but *when*. However, this could lead some to wonder whether we actually have a say in the matter. Are we really free to choose?

Yes, we are. Every child was raised by an imperfect person, so we could all try to blame our shortcomings and failures on our parents. But when a father who was abused in his youth later abuses his own child, do we excuse his actions on account of his troubled upbringing? Of course not. A court of law would never entertain such a defense—and neither should God. Even serial killer Jeffrey Dahmer had this to say regarding his own actions:

> I feel it's wrong for people who commit crimes to try to
> shift the blame onto somebody else, onto their parents

or onto their upbringing or living circumstances. I think that's just a cop-out. ... They're absolutely not responsible for any of it in any way, and I take full responsibility.[2]

We are responsible for our decisions and we know it. It is because we can discern right from wrong that we conceal our depraved acts from others. This shows we are fully capable of controlling our actions, yet choose not to. But the most compelling evidence for freedom of choice lies in the future judgments of God, which promise wrath for some and reward for others. It would be completely unjust for God to punish or reward a creature if he had no choice in his decisions and was simply acting as a robot.

Mundane decisions have little bearing on our lives. Deciding which socks to wear carries no moral weight. But all the heavier issues in life will require us to choose between right and wrong. Each person's circumstances present unique trials of an ethical nature. All will encounter such forks in the road, and it is then that our choices matter most.

The path we choose—and even the paths chosen by those around us—can make it easier (or more difficult) for us to find or accept the truth in this life. It may carry us closer to or further from God. Our decisions have the potential to make us perfectly content or absolutely miserable. We have the power to choose the type of life we are constructing for ourselves and those around us. Not only do those decisions affect us now, but we will also be held responsible for them later—perhaps particularly the burdens our selfish behavior has brought upon others.

MAN'S WILL VERSUS GOD'S

Freedom to choose gives us ample opportunity to enjoy this life or wreck it. We have control. We imagine ourselves totally free. It may feel as though we are operating independently, beyond the influence of outside forces, but this is only an illusion. Whether by circumstance or lack of power, we are clearly restrained. There are many inherent limitations in life that lie outside the realm of choice: We can't defy the laws of gravity. We can't select our ethnicity. We are not really free to become as wealthy, famous, intelligent, or beautiful as we please. We can't just decide to live forever. And we can't cure ourselves of sin, or earn salvation.[3] Even being born wasn't our choice. We are all on this roller coaster called life, though no one chose to climb aboard. Now that we are on it, we can raise our arms, scream, cover our eyes, or open them wide—but ultimately the ride goes where the track was laid, and there's absolutely nothing we can do to change its course. Because our potential actions are limited, our freedom to choose will lead to a narrow range of outcomes.

That means our decisions must be fairly predictable. Given our genetic makeup, past life experiences, and circumstances at any given moment, we are guaranteed to make our particular choice with mathematical certainty. We would probably even make the same exact decisions as those we've criticized, had we been dealt the same body, mind, and circumstances. This does not excuse their poor choices, nor suggest they won't be held responsible. It merely indicates we would perform no better at their life than they have—which may be why God warned us not to judge each other.[4] All of us are flawed.[5]

The sphere of our free choice has been likened to that of a novice chess player challenging a skilled master. Man feels totally free to make his own decisions, but God can easily checkmate him at any time. Life, like a chess board, offers what appear to be infinite paths to choose from, but there are limits. The master sees a narrow and discrete set of possibilities to plan his next move. God can simply present circumstances that leave no desirable alternative, leading us to choose the very same option he wills.[6] In a few short moves, we may find ourselves longing to do exactly what God desired. This strategy doesn't subvert our freedom to choose, but it does pare down the list of favorable options we are willing to consider. God can influence the game if he needs to, and sometimes he does.

The notion that man's freedom of choice could ever frustrate the will of God is preposterous. Nonetheless, this is what many modern Christians teach. Seemingly unaware that this is the quintessential god complex, they fancy themselves the powerful designers of their own fates, unrestrained by external forces. But directing our steps is trivial. When hungry, we eat. To avoid a collision, we brake. If a storm is coming, we take cover. God can control these circumstances. Sure, we remain free to choose, but that freedom exists within the realm of God's sovereign control. He is free to choose too—and this includes using our decisions to shape the final outcome to his will.[7]

God doesn't need to use force to win his enemies. True love can't be forced from anyone; it can only be elicited by loving them first. Once the truth of his unconditional love and boundless grace is revealed to all, every last person will gladly embrace God. All rational creatures will choose in their own self-interest, and God, who is central to our composition, is precisely what we were designed to seek. Inevitably, all will side with the truth.

While we are free to choose our own path, the most important outcome of all—the fate of his creation—is something God is sure to influence. Mankind has made a lot of bad moves, but God has masterfully checkmated us in a way that guarantees we will share in his victory. God doesn't lose.

NEITHER DEATH NOR LIFE

All things were created by God, including death. It exists for a limited time to serve a purpose, and he has complete control over it. While we may see death as permanent, God has the power to give life or take it from any creature he wishes.[8]

Modern Christian teachings suggest that if a person is not saved before he dies, he is irreversibly sent to hell for endless torment. But if this were true, a person whose life is taken early, before having a chance to hear of Christ, would be lost forever. This would effectively hand mankind the unimaginable power to send anyone to hell forever simply by killing them early in life. This cannot be. The trite answer to this dilemma is that "God knows whether they would have chosen to believe."

And what about a young child who dies too early to confess that Jesus is Lord? Many teach that those who die before reaching the "age of accountability" will be taken straight to paradise. But where in the Bible is an age of accountability mentioned? It isn't.

Like so many dubious doctrines that have worked their way into today's Christianity, these canned answers find no support whatsoever in the Scriptures. These coping mechanisms were created to soften the horrors of eternal torment, and to give God a chance to overcome untimely deaths.

Every person is destined to die. Our lives are compared to water spilled on the ground, which cannot be gathered up again. God assures us he does not simply take life away, but devises ways to draw men back to avoid separation from him.[9] God loves every member of his creation just the same a day before his death as the day after. Jesus remains the same yesterday, today, and forever.[10]

Although death is our enemy, it finally brings an end to dying. It allows the believer to be made new. Death is not a reason to abandon hope. It is not the end. And it will never separate us from the love of God:

> For I am sure that neither death nor life, nor angels nor rulers, nor things present nor things to come, nor powers, nor height nor depth, nor anything else in all creation, will be able to separate us from the love of God in Christ Jesus our Lord. (Romans 8:38–39 NIV)

Jesus' resurrection demonstrated his power over death. The Holy Spirit that restored his life is the same one that dwells inside the heart of each believer, and will ultimately raise them from the dead in the same way.[11] Death is the last enemy Jesus will destroy, after which the state of mortality will necessarily cease to exist altogether. Death and dying will no longer be possible. Abundant life for every member of creation—full, fearless, endless life—is all that can remain once this promise is fulfilled.

No one can derail God's ultimate victory, even if they die while rejecting the truth. Death and hell are no obstacles for Jesus. He holds the keys to both:

> "Fear not, I am the first and the last, and the living one. I died, and behold I am alive forevermore, and I have the keys of Death and Hades." (Revelation 1:17–18 ESV)

Many modern Christians seem to think Jesus is going to guard these keys forever—like the warden of a prison—to permanently seal the fate of those gripped by death and hell. Is that what victory looks like? I don't think so.

As Brad Jersak puts it: If Jesus holds the keys to Death and Hades, what do you think he'll do with them?[12]

CHAPTER 18

TIME

*It is by no means an irrational fancy that,
in a future existence, we shall look upon what we think
our present existence, as a dream.*

— EDGAR ALLAN POE

TIME did not exist until a physical universe came to be. Since God created the universe, we could say he existed "before" time. God's existence transcends time. He isn't limited to or bound by its constraints; he created it. For us, however, there is no escape from the clutches of time. It is essential to our understanding. We envision a linear timeline of events, and speak in terms of past, present, or future. We recognize that time cannot be revisited once it has passed, which gives our decisions finality and consequence. We know our time here will one day end.

Our lives can be divided into stages of development. First, as a baby, we are completely dependent upon caretakers. Next we become toddlers, experiencing our first taste of freedom through mobility. As a child, we begin to consider the consequences of our actions. The adolescent age is marked by rapid physical change and a bit of chaos. As young adults, many of us begin to realize that we are, in fact, mortal. Later, as adults, we navigate careers and relationships with what is often sloppy judgment. And finally, as a senior, our focus turns to coping with all the physical ailments we collected along the way. Hopefully by then we have figured out what is truly important in life, and have begun to pursue it. It takes a lifetime to grow up and progress through each stage.

The progression of mankind as a whole is similar. In fact, God has divided the existence of humanity into various time periods as well. The sequence of these stages sheds light on his plan for us. At each step along the way, mankind's focus has been shifted slightly to bring about greater maturity and understanding.

LOST IN TRANSLATION

Unfortunately we might miss this concept completely if we relied only on the familiar old King James Version of the Bible. In fact, some of the most priceless insight into God's message for mankind is difficult to find because many translations have butchered the original meanings of key words. Remember how "love" in English can represent various different Greek words? There is a similar debacle in Hebrews:

> For then must he often have suffered since the foundation of the *world* [Greek: κόσμου]: but now once in the end of the *world* [Greek: αἰώνων] hath he appeared to put away sin by the sacrifice of himself. (Hebrews 9:26 KJV)

Table 18.1. *Words translated as "world" in Hebrews 9:26*

ORIGINAL	TRANSLIT.	ROOT MEANING	KJV RENDERING
κόσμου	kosmos	world	world
αἰώνων	aiōnion	age	world

The English word "world" appears twice in this translation of the verse. The first instance is the Greek word *kosmos*, but the second comes from the root word *aiōn*.[1] Surely the original author chose to use two entirely different words for a reason.[2] Why, then, are they both translated "world"?

The first instance of *world* is correct, since *kosmos*—just like the English word "cosmos"—refers to the world or universe. But the second word means something else entirely: *aiōn*, like "eon," refers to an age or period of time. It's not a "world" at all.

Some translations have since attempted to address this glaring inconsistency. For instance, in the New International Version, the second "world" is changed to the more accurate *ages*:

> Otherwise Christ would have had to suffer many times since the creation of the *world*. But he has appeared once for all at the culmination of the *ages* to do away with sin by the sacrifice of himself. (Hebrews 9:26 NIV)

Much better. It's important to note that most people select a Bible translation without realizing discrepancies like this exist between them. While this example may seem a fairly innocuous change on the surface, decisions like these, made entirely by translators, have led to disastrous interpretations.

Most of the damage inflicted by faulty translations stems from this same Greek word *aiōn* and its derivatives. This word is critical to understanding God's plan for mankind. Of the 128 times it appears, the King James Version renders it *ever* (71 times), *world* (38 times), *never* (6 times), *evermore* (4 times), *age* (2 times), *eternal* (2 times), and five others. But each of these words mean very different things, and some of them are even opposites. How can a single word be translated as *ever*, *never*, *temporal*, *everlasting*, and *eternal* all in the same book? The Hebrew word *owlam*, which is equivalent to the Greek *aiōn*, suffers the same mistreatment.

It's also troubling that the original Greek word appears in both singular and plural forms, yet nowhere do we find it translated "evers," "eternals," or "forevers." Why not? Further, references are made to times before and after an *aiōn*, so it clearly describes something with a beginning and an end—not "forever." Did the translators render each word consistently and accurately, or did they make choices that fit their theology?

AN ETERNAL MESS

"Eternal" is one of the most abused words in the English language. It describes something that has no beginning and no end. Laymen often mistakenly use the phrase "eternal life" with regard to the afterlife. But how could a human, who did not exist before birth, ever participate in anything *eternally*? This is impossible. We could certainly enjoy "everlasting life," "endless life," or even "live forever." But to have *eternal* life, one would need to have existed before time began. They would have to be timeless—yet nothing is timeless except for God. For this reason, proper use of "eternal" is almost exclusively limited to God and his qualities, such as his power or righteousness.[3]

Unfortunately, the same mistake is likely found throughout your Bible: the word "eternal" appears forty-seven times in the King James Version, and a whopping *eighty* times in the New International Version—yet most instances clearly do not refer to God. Which translation is infallible?

The English words "forever" and "everlasting" are similarly misused. In the King James Version they are repeatedly applied to things that are unquestionably temporary. For example, Jonah is trapped "forever," only to be released three days later.[4] We are told of a slave who will serve his master "forever," yet would die like every other man.[5] Solomon built a temple for God to dwell in "forever," but the temple was destroyed 400 years later.[6] Aaron and his sons were anointed to "everlasting" priesthood, which was later canceled.[7] The original word clearly means "for an age," and refers to an indefinite period of time.[8] It may have been three days, or many generations—but each denotes a finite period of time with a beginning and an end.

Translators obviously recognize the problem, because they avoid using "everlasting" or "eternity" in verses like Romans 12:2. "Do not conform to the pattern of this *eternity*" doesn't work, so many versions casually replace it with "world" instead. Sounds better, but it's wrong—the original word is based on *aiōn*, not *kosmos*. Don't take my word for it; look it up yourself.

Matthew 13:39, 13:49, 24:3, and 28:20 all refer to "the end of" an age. While the New International Version typically translates *aiōn* as "forever" or "everlasting," it simply wouldn't work in these verses: the "end of forever" is nonsense, so the translators had little choice but to correctly render it *age*. Similarly, the original Greek in 1 Corinthians 2:7 refers to a time "before the ages." The NIV doesn't read "before the *forever*" or "before *eternity*," since that would be ridiculous. Instead, the translators settled on "before time began," which still misses the point.

Many versions render Revelation 11:15 to say Christ will reign "for ever and ever"—again, words based on *aiōn*.[9] However, this interpretation contradicts 1 Corinthians 15:25–28, which clearly states that Christ must reign *until* he puts all his enemies under his feet, after which Jesus himself will then be subject to God. Jesus will *not* rule forever. This is why more accurate translations read "to the ages of the ages" instead. What does yours say?

For those who still think phrases like "ages of the ages" might mean forever, consider this: Have you ever once thought the "holy of holies" represented infinite space? Of course not. It is simply the holiest of the areas within the tabernacle. Likewise, "ages of the ages" simply refers to a finite period within the ages—not forever, and certainly not eternity.

Clearly we don't need a full grasp of the original languages to see that modern translations contain grave errors. The contradictions are obvious. It has long been acknowledged that there are problems surrounding *aiōn* and its derivatives, which have been rendered with completely different meanings in the various

English versions. A thorough examination of the historical use of this Greek word will demonstrate conclusively that it denotes *limited* duration.[10, 11, 12] As renowned Bible scholar G. Campbell Morgan warned over a century ago,

> [L]et me say to Bible students that we must be very careful how we use the word "eternity." We have fallen into great error in our constant use of that word. There is no word in the whole Book of God corresponding with our "eternal," which, as commonly used among us, means absolutely without end. The strongest Scripture word used with reference to the existence of God, is—"unto the ages of the ages," which does not literally mean eternally.[13]

Despite warnings like this and numerous glaring inconsistencies, some translations make gratuitous use of "eternal," "forever," and "everlasting" in the wrong context, where simply referring to these periods as *ages*—as the original languages do—eliminates these contradictions, and is far more accurate.

DIVISIONS OF TIME

God created divisions of time, referred to as "ages" in the original Greek.[14] Before this, the ages did not exist.[15] Jesus spoke of a future period he called the "age to come."[16] Though time will continue to pass, at some point the ages will end.[17] Obviously God has divided time into an unknown number of ages. What for?

Just as a person's life can be divided into stages from infant to senior, the timeline of mankind as a whole appears to have been divided into ages that represent God's dealings with man. Each subsequent period of development is designed to bring about greater maturity and insight into his plan. Some put the number of divisions at three, five, or even more than a dozen. The following table contains some of the more commonly identified ages humanity is thought to progress through:

Table 18.2. *Possible divisions of the ages*

EON	TITLE	SIGNIFICANCE
1	Ignorance	Innocence in the Garden of Eden
2	Conscience	Knowledge of good and evil
3	Covenant	Promises made to Abraham
4	Law	Laws provided through Moses
5	Grace	The present age of self-governance
6	Kingdom	Christ's thousand-year reign on earth
7	Future	At least one additional future age

Many efforts have been made to define the ages, but the Bible does not enumerate an authoritative list. However, it is clear that God dealt with us differently when he walked with Adam in the garden, as compared to today. Circumstances have changed many times throughout history, and these periods illustrate how God has advanced mankind's development by bringing us through each stage: ignorance in our infancy; introduction of knowledge of good and evil; the promise of future blessings; the rule of law and the provision of governing authority to establish order; the age of grace ushered in by Christ; the future reign of Christ; and at least one more future age, as described in Ephesians 2:7. However they may be divided, the end of the ages will culminate in all creation being freed from its bondage to sin and decay.[18] This is God's plan and the purpose of the ages.[19]

As a child grows older, we expect different behavior with each new stage in life. The same is to be expected of us during our progression through the ages. For instance, after Christ's perfect sacrifice was made, the laws that prescribed animal offerings were invalidated.[20] Old Testament laws, such as those that forbid eating pork in Leviticus 11:7–8, no longer apply today.[21] We should take care not to confuse messages intended for those in certain groups or ages as applicable to every reader of the Bible. God's plan and expectations never change, but our understanding and experience does with each new stage.

The Old Testament accounts of divine judgment seem rather brutal, particularly if we fail to consider the ultimate outcome for all people. But in the earliest ages, it seems God accommodated our ignorance and lack of civility by dealing with us on our level. He had to reveal himself in ways we could understand. God's presence, accessibility, and direct involvement with our immature ancestors necessitated swift intervention at times. A good parent never takes pleasure in punishing his children, and neither does God—but a father is expected to take action if his children are harming themselves or one another. In earlier ages, God's immediate mitigation of the most heinous works of evil—though forceful—extended mercy to the whole of mankind.

Today God does not usually deal with us so directly. Mankind has graduated to an age of self-reliance, like an adult. At this point, God's direct intervention would impinge man's liberty to forge his own way, which appears to be the purpose of this age. Modern man no longer fears divine punishment because it is so far removed from his memory. However, the latitude he now enjoys in ruling over himself in this age comes at the cost of the creator's direct guidance—along with reverence for his power—and opens the door to an increasing burden of future consequence.

And so it continues, with each stage presenting greater understanding and new challenges. Each age has provided us with unique opportunities to put forth our best efforts, fail, and long for a better future—a cure we are unable to bring about ourselves through works, medicine, or technology. The ages seem crafted to demonstrate that, despite all our great achievements, we remain helpless. Our only hope is to call upon God.

CHAPTER 19

JUSTICE

At his best, man is the noblest of all animals;
separated from law and justice he is the worst.

— ARISTOTLE

G OD WILL PARDON every sin, no questions asked—but this
  might seem a little unfair. How could a vicious serial killer
be offered the same forgiveness as a sweet little old lady?

A murderer who rejects Christ will eventually be redeemed
once he confesses Jesus is Lord. His past behavior has no bearing
on this. Redemption has been secured for all creatures by the
blood of Christ.[1] What isn't as clear are the events that transpire
between his death and ultimate salvation. Many verses warn of
judgment and justice. But whatever lies ahead cannot change the
outcome of God's final victory over sin. This foretold end result
ensures that the intensity and duration of any rehabilitation must
be finite. God's promise to end all suffering and death cannot be
fulfilled until *all* struggle comes to an end.

All will come to believe in and call upon Jesus as Lord and be
reconciled to God in the end. In light of this, some may wonder
what difference it makes to believe now. What does the future

hold for believers versus unbelievers? Both will die. Both will be resurrected.[2] And both will be judged.[3] But the timing and circumstances of these events will be different for each group.

Near the end of the present age, Jesus Christ will return to earth. At that moment, those who placed their faith in him in this life will take part in what is called the *first resurrection*.[4] All dead believers will be awakened to life. They enjoy this status earlier than others not because they upheld high standards or resisted sin, which all fail to do. Rather, they are simply the first to see the truth: that Jesus' sinless life was the ransom paid to take away all sin and free us from bondage. Now deemed sinless, they receive a new body cured of sin and death that is incorruptible and immortal.[5] They will live forever from that moment forward in a state of perfection.[6] Believers will have the privilege of participating in the next age, often called the *millennial age*, in which Christ rules on earth for a period of one thousand years.[7]

But what about everyone else? What happens to the ancient cities destroyed for their wickedness, or all those who died in the flood? Everyone who rejected, ignored, did not hear, or failed to realize the truth within their lifetimes will remain dead for one thousand years, missing the millennial age entirely.[8] Unlike the believers, they will not yet understand what Christ has done, and are not yet ready to be redeemed. After the millennial age is over they will awaken uncured, still susceptible to and afflicted by death. Upon waking to reality and encountering Jesus Christ the creator—as Saul did—they will undoubtedly call upon him as Lord and be saved. However, each person will still need to be made new. For sin and death to be cured, the old must die—just as was required for believers.[9] Therefore those who do not take part in the first resurrection must go through a *second* death.[10]

Most English translations of John 3:16 suggest that Jesus promised "everlasting life" or "eternal life" to his followers. However, the Greek word used here is once again derived from *aiōn.* What if Jesus wasn't even talking about immortality? What if he was simply promising life for the coming age—or "life age-during," as some versions read? That would mean believers would be resurrected in the next age to live during his kingdom on earth. This aligns perfectly with other related verses.

Some will ask, "But wait, what about the promise of eternal life?" (They mean *everlasting* life, of course; only God is eternal!) Again, verses like these refer to *ages*, which are finite periods of time. We don't know how long every age will last, but we do know that they end. Life "for the age" won't last forever, but don't worry: the bigger promise is that the last enemy to be destroyed is death. Once death is abolished forever, it is impossible for any creature to die or stay dead. After this happens, *immortality is the result for all.* No one that has ever existed will remain dead, and all will live forever. It is God's victory over death that guarantees immortality, not a word that means "age."

THE CONSUMING FIRE

Many verses mention flames and fire in the context of judgment.[11] We are warned that "Every one shall be salted with fire."[12] This includes thieves, infants, killers, and sweet little old ladies. What is the point of this fire? Is it to torture God's creatures? No, the fire has a much greater purpose: correction.

Everyone who misses out on the first resurrection and the next age will rise to life and experience a *second* death.[13] The fire present at the second death is used for refinement. Just as gold is refined with fire to remove unwanted impurities called *dross*, God will purify mankind to remove all that ails us.[14] All deception and every obstacle to seeing the truth will be destroyed, allowing all to freely embrace Jesus as Lord. God has promised the people of Israel, "I will thoroughly purge away your dross and remove all your impurities."[15] Given that these are God's chosen people, the goal is clearly to *improve*—not simply to torment.[16]

Fire does not harm pure gold or change its composition. Likewise, the resurrected believers will be impervious to the fire of the second death, as it only affects those in need of a cure. Lives that have collected few impurities may need very little refinement, while others may require some extra passes. Facing true reality may be amazing for some, while terribly painful for others. But the soul, like gold, is never harmed by fire. Only the waste—evil, pride, sinful thoughts—is burned up and destroyed. God purifies us by stripping all the junk away, which puts us back closer to the way we were designed to be. Closer to the image of God.

Few would object to a creator that punishes his creatures for their heinous crimes, but punishing them *forever* makes no sense. Discipline that continues regardless of any improvement is not discipline at all—it's senseless torture. If God's discipline doesn't succeed in correcting a person, then it fails to benefit them. And failing doesn't bring glory to God. Thankfully, God isn't a sore loser whose only remaining option is to inflict endless pain. He's in the business of *winning*.

Standing in stark contrast to the twisted modern pop-theology of endless hell is God's magnificent *redemptive* purpose behind the fire of judgment. But perhaps the most interesting part is that God explicitly tells us that he "is a consuming fire."[17] So it isn't blind vengeance or the fire of wrath, but *an encounter with God* that purifies us. God is love, and we are the objects of his love. And though it may be painful, the Great Physician will do whatever it takes to cure all disease, rebellion, and deception—both for our benefit and to his glory.[18] God's character demands that his discipline serve a logical, corrective function: it must *fix* us, and then come to an end. Every effort to heal or cure or fix or correct must result in success, otherwise *God has failed*.

To be clear, discipline does not in itself bring about salvation. Judgment saves no one. Salvation comes solely through belief and confession that Jesus is Lord. Once our impurities are purged, all obstacles are removed—each person is then able to see and embrace God's truth and freely call upon the Christ.

THE LAKE OF FIRE, HELL, AND THE GRAVE

Many misleading sermons invoke the *lake of fire* described in the Book of Revelation. Many mainstream Christians teach that it represents endless misery, or a "hell" akin to *Dante's Inferno*. But what does the Bible really say regarding this future event?

> And the sea gave up the dead which were in it; and death and hell delivered up the dead which were in them: and they were judged every man according to their works. And death and hell were cast into the lake of fire. This is the second death. And whosoever was not found written in the book of life was cast into the lake of fire.[19]

At the final judgment, everything that isn't pure will be cast into a lake of fire. Hell will be "cast into the lake of fire." But if the lake of fire *is* hell—as we are often told—then how could God cast hell into... hell? Obviously these two things cannot be the same.

A lake filled with fire may evoke images of the pagan concept of hell, but we've already seen what fire represents: the purifying judgment of the eternal God. Daniel 7:10 describes a flood of fire flowing forth from God as he takes his place upon the throne of judgment. It is the fire of divine perfection. It is coming face to face with the Creator, which forces anything impure to surface and be burned up, leaving behind only that which has value.

What, then, is meant by *hell*? The words usually translated as "hell" in modern Bibles are *sheol* (Hebrew) and *hades* (Greek).[20] First, these two words are exactly equal. We know this because Acts 2:25–28, written in Greek, is a direct quote of Psalm 16:8–11, which is in Hebrew. Both passages read "For thou wilt not leave my soul in hell" in two different languages, so each word clearly has the same meaning. Second, this passage was penned by King David, whom God describes as "a man after my heart, who will do

all my will.["21] David is certainly not destined for endless agony; if
he can't escape it, no one can! Third, this psalm was a prophetic
reference to the coming messiah, Jesus Christ, which it calls the
"Holy One." Few are willing to suggest that Christ himself has
been abandoned in fiery torment.

The original meaning of the words *sheol* and *hades* has been
warped by pagan mythology and careless translators to represent
a place of anguish. But it is merely a condition both King David
and Jesus could be found in: *the grave*. The King James Version
correctly renders *sheol* as "grave" thirty-one times throughout the
Old Testament. Sinners and saints alike will end up there. Note
that this word isn't an attempt to describe a specific location, but
a state: the unseen state of being dead instead of alive. It is by no
means a punishment.

Table 19.1. *Words rendered "hell" in the King James Version*

ORIGINAL	LANGUAGE	MEANING	"GRAVE"	"HELL"
sheol	Hebrew	grave; unseen	31 times	31 times
hades	Greek	grave; unseen	1 time	10 times

At the future event witnessed in Revelation 20:13–15, death and
hades "delivered up the dead which were in them." After this, both
are cast into the lake of fire to be completely consumed, never to
return. Once these things have taken place, no one can possibly
remain dead or in the grave. Death and the grave will have served
their purpose, and no longer have any value.

So whatever anyone thinks *hades* represents, of this we can be
certain: it will be emptied and then cease to exist in the future.
And the second death must also end, because 1 Corinthians 15:26
reveals that at the end of the ages, "the last enemy to be destroyed
is death." Death in all forms will eventually be eradicated. This
includes the second death.

DEATH MEANS WE DIE

Today's Christian leaders are tragically misinformed regarding death. They say "heaven" is a place with gold streets where saints live now; that "hell" is a fiery place of anguish separated from God; and that as soon as we "die" we are immediately relocated to one of these two places. In other words, *we never die.*

But this flatly contradicts the Scriptures. David himself "did not ascend to heaven" according to Acts 2:29–34. Death is equated to sleep, which is the state 1 Thessalonians 4:13–16 tells us all Old Testament saints are in now. As William Tyndale questioned in the sixteenth century, why would "the dead in Christ" rise to life in the first resurrection if they are already alive?[22] Ecclesiastes 9:10 clearly tells us that in the grave "there is neither working nor planning nor knowledge nor wisdom." David himself states in Psalm 6:5 that among the dead, "no one proclaims your name. Who praises you from the grave?" As Martin Luther, father of the Protestant Reformation, observed:

> Solomon judgeth that the dead are asleep, and feel nothing at all. For the dead lie there counting neither days nor years, but when they are awoken, they shall seem to have slept scarce one minute.[23]

In the garden of Eden, the serpent lied to the woman, "You will not surely die." Similarly, most churches today tell us we won't really be dead when we die—but the Bible suggests otherwise.

Few realize that the Hebrew and Greek words most often translated "heaven" in modern Bibles simply mean the visible sky above.[24] If by *heaven* we really mean "paradise with God," we must acknowledge that the Holy City with pearly gates foretold in Revelation doesn't exist yet: it is yet to be established, since we are explicitly told it will be right here on earth.[25] And if by *hell* we really mean "the lake of fire," we must also acknowledge that it won't appear until the future judgment. So it becomes clear that heaven and hell, as we've come to understand them based on traditional folklore, *don't exist yet.* So no one is in them. And why would they be, without first being judged?

Despite all the evidence, the fact that we are actually *dead* when we die is largely unknown among Christians today. This can be a difficult topic for some. It can be uncomfortable to consider that our loved ones may not be strumming harps in the clouds as we've been told. But would we really want them to witness the horrible things going on today? Would they want to watch us suffer? Or are they simply asleep for a time, just as the Bible describes?

The modern teaching that the soul is immortal is contradictory and unbiblical. It robs Jesus of the honor he is due for defeating death and bringing us back to life. Apart from Christ, there is no life. Only he gave us life for the ages, and only he can raise us to a final state of becoming immortal and incorruptible.

THE PURPOSE OF JUDGMENT

In Exodus chapter 3, Moses encounters God within a bush that is on fire but never burns up. Likewise, the fire of divine judgment will consume all that is impure and preserve all that God values. It will not destroy the person:

> Every man's work shall be made manifest: for the day shall declare it, because it shall be revealed by fire; and the fire shall try every man's work of what sort it is. If any man's work abide which he hath built thereupon, he shall receive a reward. If any man's work shall be burned, he shall suffer loss: but he himself shall be saved; yet so as by fire. (1 Corinthians 3:13–15)

God's judgments reveal the true value of our good deeds based on our motives, for which we may be rewarded.[26] For instance, believers who have made good use of their talents in this age will be given greater responsibilities in the next.[27] In giving rewards, God is able to recognize those who have freely chosen to live for him. Rewards do not confer or confirm superiority. In fact, even our rewards from God belong to him.[28] And every person—even those who actively worked to stifle his kingdom—will still receive the greatest gift of all: reconciliation.

God's goal is to refine and correct mankind.[29] He may pour out wrath in judgment, but only to make things right.[30] He may let us do things our own way for a short time, but God's mercy will be great when he gathers all men to himself.[31]

THE DURATION OF GOD'S DISCIPLINE

The fallacy of endless torment is refuted by the finality of God's future victory against sin and death. The unequivocal clarity of these promises rises above the murky waters of translation, clear beyond question. However, to be certain, we will also examine the most commonly cited passages offered to purportedly prove that at least part of mankind will be tormented forever.

Each is from the King James Version, with alternate renderings from Young's Literal Translation appearing in brackets. Neither version is presented as authoritative, but were simply selected to illustrate vast differences in interpretation on a doctrine that is still taught dogmatically as if it were never in doubt.

UNQUENCHABLE FIRE (MARK 9:43–48)

> And if thy hand offend thee, cut it off: it is better for thee to enter into life maimed, than having two hands to go into hell [*literally "to the Gehenna"*], into the fire that never shall be quenched: Where their worm dieth not, and the fire is not quenched.

The word translated "hell" here is actually *Geenna* (or *Gehenna*), which represents Hinnom, a valley south of Jerusalem where dead animals and trash were burned. Many translations conflate *sheol* and *hades*—the grave—with *Geenna*, indiscriminately rendering them all as "hell" more than fifty times. But this word, appearing

only twelve times, does not represent the grave (the unseen state
of the dead). It refers to a physical place of judgment on earth
named Hinnom.[32] Verses that contain this word describe being
cast into the fire of God's judgment, similar to the lake of fire.
This valley could well be the actual location of the future lake of
fire—right here on earth, just outside Jerusalem.

There is no denying that serious correction lies ahead for some.
God's aim is perfection, and we are far from it. The unquenchable
fire of his judgment will burn away all impurity. Because God *is*
the consuming fire, the fire is eternal in nature. However, it does
not logically follow from this verse that God will punish anyone
endlessly; or that God's judgments serve no corrective purpose;
or that God's corrective discipline will fail to fix us. Each of these
would violate at least one of God's promises.

ASCENDING SMOKE (REVELATION 14:11)

> And the smoke of their torment ascendeth up for ever and
> ever [*literally "to ages of ages"*]: and they have no rest
> day nor night, who worship the beast and his image, and
> whosoever receiveth the mark of his name.

The words rendered "for ever and ever" are based on *aiōn*, which
again means "eon" or "age."[33] In this case it is plural, so if this
word truly meant eternity, the passage should read "for eternities
and eternities"—but that clearly makes no sense.[34] More accurate
translations read "to ages of ages," which simply indicates this
period of correction spans multiple ages, not that it is endless.

SHAME AND CONTEMPT (DANIEL 12:2)

> And many of them that sleep in the dust of the earth shall
> awake, some to everlasting life [*literally "life age-during"*],
> and some to shame [*literally "reproaches"*] and everlasting
> [*literally "age-during"*] contempt.

Again, our modern English translations suffer from a deep

misapprehension of the original Greek term which represents an age. Obviously if anyone were to feel shame or contempt *forever*, God's promise to subject all things to Christ so that God can become All in all would never be fulfilled.

FROM HIS PRESENCE (2 THESSALONIANS 1:9)

> Who shall be punished with everlasting destruction [*literally "shall suffer justice—destruction age-during"*] from the presence of the Lord, and from the glory of his power.

We are often told unbelievers will be separated from God forever. In reality, punishment is brought about by the *presence* of God. The Greek word *prosōpon* here means "face."[35] Ironically, those being punished are brought before the *face* of God—not separated from him—to witness his limitless power and glory, and behold what they could not see before.

Regardless, the word rendered "everlasting" is derived from *aiōn*, and therefore refers to an eon or age—simply a period of correction. It would be completely unjust for God's discipline to be everlasting without end.

THE SHEEP AND GOATS (MATTHEW 25:31–46)

> Then shall he say also unto them on the left hand, 'Depart from me, ye cursed, into everlasting fire [*literally "to the fire, the age-during"*], prepared for the Devil and his angels. ... And these shall go away into everlasting punishment [*literally "punishment age-during"*]: but the righteous into life eternal [*literally "life age-during"*].

The translators continue to fumble the ages, arbitrarily rendering three instances of the *same exact word* as "everlasting" twice and "eternal" once, as though these were interchangeable. All three correctly refer to an age in Young's Literal Translation.

Also, the Greek word rendered "punishment" is *kolasin*, which represents discipline intended to correct the subject. It is a word derived from *kolazō*, which means "pruning," as in gardening. This is clearly distinguished from other available Greek words that represent vengeance wrought merely to satisfy the torturer, with no intent to cure.[36]

We know that salvation is not based on our behavior.[37] So it is extraordinarily important to note that this passage, which is often cited as proof of endless torment, describes judgment *based on works*. In other words, the consequences it describes cannot possibly be the result of failing to believe in Jesus. In fact, this particular passage depicts Christ's judgment of the *nations* at his throne—not individuals—and is based on how they treated the poor and the powerless, not whether they believed.

THE RICH MAN AND LAZARUS (LUKE 16:23–31)

> And in hell [*literally "hades"*] he lift up his eyes, being in torments, and seeth Abraham afar off, and Lazarus in his bosom. And he cried and said, Father Abraham, have mercy on me, and send Lazarus, that he may dip the tip of his finger in water, and cool my tongue; for I am tormented in this flame.

This passage is frequently offered in support of endless torment. However, three critical points must be noted.

First, there is no indication that this condition is *endless*, and in fact there is no mention of time at all. There's no reason the circumstances described couldn't eventually bring about a better outcome through God's corrective discipline.

Second, the story describes the consequences visited upon two different men *based on their works*. If this were the criteria used, then the decision to help the needy (or walk past them) would be what determines our afterlife, rather than faith in Christ.

Third, regardless of what it depicts, this is merely one of five stories Jesus told that day. We know that "Jesus spoke all these things to the crowd in parables; he did not say anything to them without using a parable."[38] Did you believe the prodigal son was an actual person that ate pig feed before returning to his father? That a shepherd had exactly 100 sheep and went to find the one he lost? Of course not. All of these were understood to be parables. This is why both Strong's Definitions and Thayer's Greek Lexicon refer to Lazarus as "imaginary."[39]

This story illustrates a fabled afterlife in which all inhabitants, both saved and unsaved, go to the same location. There they are able to see and speak to each other, but are separated by a wide chasm.[40] Based on this, some maintain that death is actually a state of conscious life, in which full awareness is experienced.[41] Insight into the afterlife cannot be gleaned from this parable, as it was actually intended to warn the Pharisees of their piety, not describe heaven or hell.

However, let's just assume for a moment that this story *is* an accurate literal description of the afterlife. If so, we are forced to conclude that everyone who dies will coexist in the same realm, in full view of one another: A loving mother on the happy side will cry out across the chasm for her lost daughter on the fiery side. Both are forever visible to one another—an inescapable reminder of all that was lost. How could this mother ever find rest? How could God bear to witness this endless misery? Surely he would be equally tormented. Thankfully, this cannot possibly be the final outcome, as it would directly contradict God's promise to destroy Satan, sin, and death.

Other passages have been cited in defense of endless torment, but these are among the most common.[42] The original text has been clouded by poor translations that for years relied heavily on Latin Vulgate and Old English versions. Old traditions die hard, but fortunately some newer revisions have been forced to address glaring errors. The truth will always prevail.

FREE TO CHOOSE

In an attempt to soften the horrific injustice of endless torment, C. S. Lewis once proposed that the doors of hell may be locked from the inside, and that rebellious people might choose to remain there forever.[43] (We will, for the sake of argument, overlook his use of the term "hell," and assume Lewis refers to the lake of fire rather than the grave.) His theory focused on free will.

However, no rational being would choose endless torment of their own volition. Only a creature *designed* to be irrational—and unnaturally so, by his creator—could choose to endure anguish without end. And despite any suggestion to the contrary, biblical depictions of judgment assure us it will be thoroughly unpleasant. It will be impossible for man to mistakenly choose torment over bliss, or fail to appreciate the difference—unless, of course, he was specifically created to do so. If a man's sinful condition is what prevents him from seeing the truth, how would it be just for God to punish him for failing to realize he needs help? Further, this contradicts God's promise that all will come to know the truth.

It defies logic and offends the conscience to suggest that God would be willing to bring any creature into existence knowing it would experience endless grief. Consider the adversary: If he is a rational creature, then God's promise to make all things new *requires* he be cured. Further, it would violate every conceivable definition of love and justice to create a being God knew would completely lack perfection, and then proceed to punish it endlessly for fulfilling that role.

Compared with our omniscient God, man is nearly oblivious to the reality around us. Our warped concept of justice is lacking. Even so, we know what is right. The near-universal laws of men charge those who abuse or neglect animals with criminal conduct. A father who does the same to his children will most certainly be prosecuted. Would a just and loving father value his child's "freedom to choose" over protecting their life? Would he let go of their hand at a busy intersection, when he knows his child will be struck by traffic and killed? Never. Yet this is just like God and man: God gets it, but mankind has no idea what hangs in the balance. Is God going to simply let go of our hand, in order to preserve some sacred "freedom to choose"? Or does he love each of us enough to hold on tightly?

Unlike earthly parents, God is the only father capable of truly *curing* his children of the very condition that prevents them from making a better choice. Is the time of our greatest need precisely the moment at which we can expect God to alienate us *forever?* Of course not. A time is coming when God will reveal what Jesus has done for us. All will see what could have been, and what we can become—and we will long to be made whole. Then Christ, the only one who can, will make it so.

FEAR STUNTS GROWTH

When threatened, a child will usually submit and behave as they are told. However, obedience based on fear comes at the expense of trust, respect, and admiration. Fear may elicit submission, but it doesn't trigger a response of love. In fact, force and fear often lead to rebellion.

Long before Jesus, men witnessed the powerful works of God. This led to a healthy fear of God, which is called "the beginning of wisdom."[44] But fear isn't wisdom. Criminals follow orders from a gang leader out of fear. Likewise, many choices and religious views are formed on threat of judgment. This can hardly be called a relationship, and doesn't necessarily reflect wisdom.

The truth is that fear is an impediment to trust. It robs us of peace. Fear severely stunts a relationship, and can prevent one altogether. Some insist that God will abandon those who don't nail the perfect formula, do good deeds, get baptized, or donate a certain portion of money. Such teachings leave many mired in legalism, trying to secure salvation, or working tirelessly to pacify a fickle tyrant. But God is love. Once we realize this, our fears will subside because

> There is no fear in love. But perfect love drives out fear, because fear has to do with punishment. The one who fears is not made perfect in love. (1 John 4:18 NIV)

In reality, fear is incompatible with true love. If we fear God, it is simply because we don't know him well enough. Fortunately, God has revealed his limitless love for us through Jesus. This should alleviate all our fears.[45] In their place will grow respect, admiration, wonder... and *love:* love for God and love for all his people, just as we were commanded.[46]

Once we are no longer operating in fear, we are free to live for God. We aren't simply trying to avoid consequences. The purity of our motives is no longer at issue. Were we to donate our time, talent, or money to show love to others, it is simply a natural response to God's unending love for us. Unfortunately, many have embraced their religious beliefs for fear of everlasting torment, and are still struggling with anxiety for themselves or their loved ones. Once they discover who God really is, this fear will vanish, and God's love will set them free.

PERFECT JUSTICE

Many mainstream Christians teach that unbelievers will forever be tormented in a fiery netherworld by Satan. Yet Hebrews 2:14 promises Satan will one day be made powerless. This presents some questions: Once Satan is no longer in charge, who will run the torture chamber? Will God take the helm as warden? Will he forever ensure the flames are turned up hot enough to make them suffer properly? If you were in control, wouldn't you at least *try* to achieve a better outcome?

Those who insist that God's justice demands this outcome "since God can't look upon sin" seem to have forgotten that he came to earth to spend all his time with sinners! What is just? Genesis 18:25 asks, "Shall not the Judge of all the earth do right?" It is telling that God invites us to apply our own concept of justice. What we deem fair should shape our expectations of God. Curious people consider this same question every day, and many are concluding that the strange brand of "justice" peddled by today's most popular Christian teachers is in fact diabolical. And they're right—endless torment isn't justice at all. These people haven't heard the good news yet: God represents *true* justice. His discipline is designed to heal us and bring great joy in the end.[47]

Justice has a corrective intent. It would be unjust to sentence a man to unlimited punishment for a limited number of offenses committed within his brief lifetime. Whether it lasts one hundred years or even a trillion, punishment must end once the penalty is paid in full. Jesus once warned against waiting until one's day in court to settle a debt, or else the judge could send a person to prison, where he would be held until the last penny was paid.[48] In his illustration, the penalty could be paid at any time, but it was better to settle immediately. Either way, the prisoner was released once he paid the price. Anything less would be unjust.

Most people are repulsed by the idea of everlasting punishment because it is a direct violation of the behavior God requires of us.[49] He commands us to forgive each other. Does God expect us to behave better than him? Why should we forgive those who hurt us, if God intends to mercilessly roast them *forever?*

Would you really be surprised to find that believers in endless torment are more willing to write off others as hopeless, cursed, or worthless—the exact opposite of what Jesus commanded?

CHAPTER 20

DARKNESS

*Progress is born of doubt and inquiry. The Church never
doubts, never inquires. To doubt is heresy, to inquire is to
admit that you do not know—the Church does neither.*

— ROBERT G. INGERSOLL

T HE POPULAR modern creed teaches that Jesus cannot or will
not save all people. That, however, is a radical departure
from the earliest Christian teachings, and flatly contradicts many
verses which unequivocally promise the salvation of all. Endless
torment has been woven into organized religion for so long that,
at least in some circles, it may seem impossible to overcome its
influence, unwise to question its validity.

During his ministry, Jesus openly criticized religious leaders; I
am confident he would be equally disappointed today. Many who
are admittedly undeserving readily accept Jesus' pardon—yet
seem to resent the idea that everyone else might receive the same
gift. Exclusivity and superiority, the very attitudes Jesus despises
most, have become the hallmarks of many of his followers.

It seems the most resistant to a message of inclusive salvation
are the leaders of modern evangelical Christianity. They often

take a hard-line stance endorsing God's everlasting punishment of the wicked. Thoughtful people would err on the side of not tarnishing his character, yet they dogmatically assure us that God will abandon most of mankind in torment forever. It is preached from the pulpit as if indisputable, yet there is no evidence to back it. Clearly, some will prefer darkness.[1] But why? If God loves us and wants us to see the truth, what is blinding us?

First, there is the human weakness of fear. We live in a world gripped by anxiety. We fear the unknown—and unfortunately for us, we know very little about the afterlife. Most believe that our destiny hinges on acceptance by the creator. It is not surprising, then, that this subject easily evokes strong emotion. Religious leaders are well aware of this. Charles H. Spurgeon, affectionately dubbed the "Prince of Preachers," admitted as much:

> I further believe, although certain persons deny it, that the influence of fear is to be exercised over the minds of men, and that it ought to operate upon the mind of the preacher himself.[2]

Fear, uncertainty, and doubt can drive men to accept and persist in ideas that have no sound basis. Many false beliefs are taught in ignorance. However, some religious concepts seem to have been purposely engineered to evoke fear of an unpleasant afterlife, since this is perhaps the most effective way to discourage people from challenging a belief system.

The second factor in spreading false beliefs is control. Our fears are easy to capitalize on. By wielding the most vicious threat of all—endless torture of the mind, body, and soul—people have proven easy to control. Since the dawn of time, the populace has willfully yielded great power and wealth to those who claim to have an inside connection with the gods. Medicine men, sages, prophets, preachers, priests—religious leaders of all types have long been endowed with what is often incontestable authority. Sincere people dutifully confess their sins, pay penance, and do as they are told, while others exploit them to gain control.[3] While the followers of these religious systems are most often pure of heart, the interjection of any mediator between God and man—other than Christ himself—is problematic. They often turn our focus away from Jesus and onto themselves.

Control doesn't have to be wicked deception. It could simply be the result of a longstanding tradition that few are willing to question so long as it continues to serve the "greater good." For instance, *If souls are being saved through fear, then so be it; the end justifies the means.* However, God has not granted us the latitude to rewrite his plan, or to hide the truth in order to make things more appealing, more frightening, or more urgent. It is what he has said; nothing more, nothing less.

Control can surface in subtle ways. A young seminary student whose personal studies lead him to see that Jesus will indeed save all people might excitedly approach his professor after class. Yet this mentor, whom he admires greatly and must please in order to graduate, responds with terse disdain. The young minister is told his thoughts are foolish, dangerous, and should be abandoned. If he wanders too far off the popular path, he won't be accepted among mainstream churches, and may find himself unemployed and unable to feed his family. This influence over the students, employees, and beneficiaries of a particular organization or its leadership grossly constrain the ability to think freely. Control may be a silent but extremely powerful force within these groups, and members feel strongly compelled to fall in line.

Paul warned us about the hollow and deceptive philosophies of men.[4] Jesus warned of religious traditions that "nullify the word of God."[5] In order for us to think clearly and critically, we must not be enslaved by fear or controlled by the influences of others. In the end, we will answer only to God—not to any other person. Our understanding should be based on the Word of God rather than the traditions of men.

GODLESS MYTHS

Fear of the unknown and thirst for control are enough to lead many people astray. But there's more to it than this. In Paul's first letter to Timothy, he acknowledged that some Christians would abandon the faith and follow false teachings.[6] This might come as quite a shock, and it should. It is unsettling to think that the church itself could be infected with bad doctrine. But as subtle changes mutate over time into something that hardly resembles the original, the results become exponentially damaging.

Was Paul referring to today's wildly popular "name it and claim it" prosperity doctrine? Maybe so. But if the adversary really wishes to undermine the gospel, perhaps the most effective way is to convince us that God doesn't value all people. That many are worthless. That God is satisfied with leaving some to burn in hell forever. But the real kicker, and the greatest insult to God, would be to get *the church itself* to spread this lie. Could there be a more effective way to sabotage the church? I doubt it.

In the same passage, Paul says everything created by God is good. This includes people. Though far from perfect, we were created in God's image, and that's enough for us to have immense value to him. Paul explicitly warns us to avoid godless myths and old wives' tales. Most importantly, he encourages us to put our hope in the living God, who is the savior of all men—especially those who believe—and tells us to command and teach these things. Which message will you share?

> Woe to those who call evil good and good evil, who put darkness for light and light for darkness. (Isaiah 5:20 NIV)

COMMON QUESTIONS

The concept of a loving God who waits patiently until all members of his creation arrive at the truth can be difficult to accept for those who have been taught otherwise all their lives. Here we address some of the questions they may have.

IF ALL ARE SAVED, WHY DID JESUS NEED TO DIE?

Imagine a man takes his family out for dinner. After all have eaten, he is told the meal is free. Does this mean that no one paid for the food? Of course not. The same is true with the gift of salvation: Even though all are ultimately saved, the ransom had to be paid. When we ask this question, we overlook the enormous price Jesus paid to remove the sin of the world and release us from bondage.

DO UNBELIEVERS GET AWAY WITH LIVING BADLY?

Some may complain, "If everyone is saved, then unbelievers get to live however they want and still get into heaven. Not fair!"

But let's be very careful. Jesus addresses this same attitude in Matthew 20:1–16 with the parable of the workers in the field. Some start their work at the beginning of the day for an agreed wage. Additional workers are then hired on throughout the day at various times—some for only an hour. At the end of the work day, all the men are paid from last to first, and all are paid the same wage. The first group complains that they did more work, and should have received more money. The landowner replies,

> "Am I not allowed to do what I choose with what belongs to me? Or do you begrudge my generosity? So the last will be first, and the first last."[7]

God can give as he pleases. If he chooses to be generous to all, who are we to argue with him? Those who hold their works in high regard will be in for quite a surprise.

This objection hints at faulty theology: A person bothered by this is likely keeping score, or may feel that they deserve a greater reward than others. They may be focused on their self-control rather than Jesus' sacrifice, or feel their works have in some way contributed. But nothing we can do—living righteously, helping others, evangelizing—will earn salvation.

Finally, this attitude suggests a fear of missing out. Those who raise this concern may feel they could be lying, cheating, stealing, and self-indulgent—but instead behave nicely because they must (for salvation) or should (for appearances). They don't seem to understand that God's intention in forbidding certain behaviors is for *their own benefit*, and that living unethically or immorally has inherent negative consequences apart from divine judgment. Do they truly believe they're being held back from enjoying life by engaging in sin? This objection suggests so.

The truth is that everyone will be tested by the fire, and all will be held accountable for their actions—both those who believe in Christ's victory now, and those who realize it later. Regardless of our opinion on the matter, God alone has the sovereign right to abundantly bless whomever he chooses, and we should rejoice.

DOES THIS UNDERMINE THE NEED TO PREACH?

If everyone will eventually be saved, some wonder why we should bother spreading the word at all. This question typically comes from believers whose relationship with God is focused almost exclusively on the afterlife. For them, there seems to be little benefit to accepting Christ as savior—no real peace, wisdom, or joy—other than a golden ticket to heaven.

It is easy to see why this attitude has become so prevalent. When we believe, as I once did, that most of humanity will rot in flames forever without any chance of escape, it can easily sap all the happiness one could hope to experience in life—and turn one's focus almost entirely to the next age.

Even though God will ultimately reconcile all of creation to himself, those who do not hear this truth miss out on the blessings it provides now. This is to say nothing of the insight gained from careful study of God's message to mankind, the rich reward of friends that share your faith, or the ability to pray to the creator of the universe. The shortsightedness of this attitude is similar to asking, "If I'm going to die anyway, why pursue an education?"

Jesus commanded believers to evangelize. God has entrusted

us with his message, and that message is the reconciliation of the entire world. Those who understand this truth are responsible for spreading the good news.[8] Since we "have been given much, much will be demanded; and from the one who has been entrusted with much, much more will be asked" (Luke 12:48 NIV).

DOES THIS MEAN GOD FORCES SALVATION UPON MEN?

Some are concerned that mankind's freedom of choice might be usurped by God. They value man's free will more than God's.

A child presented with the choice between a favorite toy or a punishment will invariably choose the toy every time. We are preprogrammed to enjoy fun. And food. And sex. These drives are not merely irresistible; they are crucial to survival. We would starve without hunger. And without reproduction, our species would cease to be. It would be preposterous to suggest that these God-given desires somehow violate our freedom to choose, since they clearly exist for our benefit.

It is equally absurd to suggest God would be "forcing himself upon us" to instill in mankind a desire to seek him. A thirst for God is no more a violation of our freedoms than the thirst for water. In fact, it would be cruel to design us *without* the single drive that leads to the cure for all pain. Yes, God gave people the freedom to choose, but he also designed us to be rational enough to know the truth when we see it. The time is coming when all obstacles to seeing reality will be removed.[9] As a result, our free choice to embrace the creator is already sealed by design.

This makes God's complete victory even more amazing: it is not achieved by force. No one can be forced into love. Neither can we choose to fall in love. Love is beyond the reach of power, above the realm of choice. It is a natural response to circumstances we do not initiate—a reaction to what we see, hear, and feel. And yet, somehow, it is the most powerful force in the universe.

All of the beauty, happiness, and comfort this world has to offer us—everything we love—was created by God. So it follows that when each of us can eventually look upon the creator who made these things for us, we will naturally love him back.[10]

God is not merely the author of love; God *is* love. Our reaction to his unfailing grace is innate and inevitable. Every man will confess Jesus is Lord to the glory of God the Father—not by force, but through clarity: all will finally see true love, and all will respond in kind. We are predestined to love our Father.

BUT ISN'T OUR FATE SEALED AT DEATH?

Some say that once we die, our destiny is sealed forever. They say it doesn't matter if we later realize Jesus is Lord because that would be too little, too late. However, this view conflicts with many clear scriptures that promise Christ's victory and mention no such terms or conditions.[11] In addition, the scriptural support for this idea hinges on *one single sentence*:

> Just as people are destined to die once, and after that to face judgment, so Christ was sacrificed once to take away the sins of many... (Hebrews 9:27–28 NIV)

If this instead read "People are destined to be born once, and after that to die," no one would suggest it means we are born and then instantly die with no time in between. Yet this is how the verse must be twisted in order to support the idea that judgment instantaneously follows death.

There is no scriptural evidence that man's death changes God's love or mercy. None. In fact, we are told the opposite: that God's love endures forever, and that he is the same yesterday, today, and forever. We may change, but God and his plan do not. We may choose to be an enemy of God, but he will not allow this to stand forever.[12] All of God's creation will ultimately worship Jesus as Lord after the truth is fully revealed to them.[13]

Since when is salvation a matter of chance? The restitution of all things is as certain as our existence. God's will is not an erratic plan that sometimes works depending on man's reaction. Salvation is guaranteed through the faithfulness of the Savior. His work done on the cross yields an irrevocable gift of grace extended to every person, whether they receive it in this age or the next.

DOES THIS MEAN HELL REFORMS MEN INSTEAD OF JESUS?

Some say the only reason unbelievers will turn to God is because they are being tried by fire, and their decision to accept Christ is only made to escape torment—something they otherwise wouldn't have done. But is this valid? After all, many Christians likely chose to accept Jesus just to avoid the very same fire.

Some laud their "wisdom" in making the right choice now, or in recognizing danger before it's too late. How quickly we forget! Grace is unmerited favor, and we contribute nothing. Either we earned it based on our choice, or salvation truly is a gift.

COULD GOD ANNIHILATE THE UNBELIEVERS?

Most agree that endless torment is incompatible with the tender mercies of a loving God. However, some insist God will permit rebellious unbelievers to have their wish—and extinguish them so they no longer exist. This is called *annihilationism.*

Annihilationism is an effort to resolve the myriad contradictions endless torment introduces, yet it fails spectacularly. It is no more compatible with a benevolent God than endless torment. How could a mother find peace in God's choice to kill off her beloved son? She would give anything to heal her son, to make him right. A hole would forever remain in her heart. Would God be okay with this outcome? Given the chance, any parent would try to do better than that. Can't God?

In order to soften the blow of losing our loved ones forever, some have suggested that our memories could be wiped from our minds so we no longer miss them. How can this be? To love someone so dearly—to invest decades of care and nurture and thought—only to have every trace removed? That sounds like a lousy cleanup plan for a creator that failed to redeem his creatures. This is by no means a victory, but an incalculable loss.

The clearest indictment against this idea is that annihilation represents permanent death or destruction. This stands in direct opposition to 1 Corinthians 15:26, which explicitly promises that death will one day be defeated. Since death won't exist, no one will be able to remain dead; annihilation will be impossible.

WHAT COULD HAVE BEEN

Studies indicate the likelihood of becoming a Christian decreases rapidly with age. Nearly half of all Americans who accept Jesus Christ as their savior do so before reaching the age of thirteen. Two out of three Christians made a commitment to Christ by age eighteen. The odds of becoming a believer after turning twenty-one are less than one in four.[14] Why is this? Are children simply more impressionable?

Jesus made it clear that children have a special connection with God.[15] It is easier for little ones to sense, with spiritual clarity, the love God has for each of us. They can open their hearts to Jesus Christ precisely because they haven't yet been tainted by our cynicism. Many are taught at a young age about the endless love of God; it is only later, nearer to adolescence, that they are indoctrinated with the dark tale of everlasting conscious torment. Evidently that's when things begin to change.

Given these statistics, I can't help but wonder: What if we were teaching the *true* gospel message instead, about a God that never gives up? One that sacrificed his only son to guarantee that *all* people would be reconciled to himself? But the modern creed is far less hopeful. Its fruits are aptly summarized by Charles Darwin, father of the theory of natural selection:

> Thus disbelief crept over me at a very slow rate, but was at last complete. ... I can indeed hardly see how anyone

ought to wish Christianity to be true; for if so the plain language of the text seems to show that the men who do not believe, and this would include my Father, Brother and almost all my best friends, will be everlastingly punished. And this is a damnable doctrine.[16]

Tragically, Mr. Darwin received a flawed message. It is, of course, no surprise that he chose to reject it. The arc of history may well have bent in a different direction altogether had we been sharing the truth of Christ's total victory instead.

Things would likely look much different today if church leaders weren't still trying to convince unbelievers to act quickly before God roasts them in flames forever. The idea is so wretched, so morally reprehensible, and so nonsensical that less people are willing to seriously entertain it. Interestingly, the same studies indicate that younger converts are less likely to believe Jesus is the only way to get to heaven, despite being unbiblical. Does this reflect an effort to reconcile childlike faith in a loving God with the twisted and contradictory modern creed? I imagine so.

Sadly, those who seem to struggle most with accepting Jesus as the Savior of all are Christians who were taught otherwise. Few appear to have researched the possibility apart from resources that parrot the safe-but-senseless popular creed, yet many will unflinchingly defend endless torment. It's a bleak reminder of our pitiful condition to see ill-informed believers insist only some will be saved based on a handful of verses, while ignoring dozens that promise the ultimate reconciliation of all. The Calvinist denies God's desire to save all; the Arminian denies God's power. Oddly, each group seems all too willing to brand as heretics those who deny neither and embrace Jesus Christ as the supreme victor. The true heresy is found in the modern church's exaltation of the will of man and Satan over God.

In a world enveloped in darkness, it can be difficult for us to comprehend the unfailing, unconditional, relentless love of God.

However, we are told that God's thoughts and his ways are higher than ours.[17] Let us listen only to what God says, and run from man's false teachings. Whatever amazing outcome you imagine, God has something far better planned—and no one can stop him from achieving it.

LOOKING FORWARD

My prayer is that you will begin to see the disconnect between today's dreadfully limited message of "hope" and the amazing promise of total victory God has written on our hearts and in his message. This is the same expectation that drove the explosive growth of the early church, and it will do the same today.

Sadly, I know many wonderful people may be concerned about whether it is safe to hope for the salvation of all; or trust in Christ's complete victory; or ask questions about God's plan for mankind. I understand the fear you may be feeling, yet I find it so incredibly tragic: This absurd and horrific teaching may be the single most effective tactic used by the adversary to undermine and discredit Christianity. It teaches that most people have no value, when in fact God considered every last one of us worth dying for. And ironically it is *the Christians themselves* who have been deceived into propagating a message rife with error that slanders God's great name and has likely prevented millions if not *billions* of reasonable people from learning more about Jesus' limitless love for them. It is time for the church to honestly confront these issues, because the rest of the world already is.

When someone gives their entire life to seeking God's heart and living out love for humanity, it seems natural to gravitate toward a gospel of victory. For example, when world-renowned evangelist Billy Graham was asked later in life whether he believed heaven will be closed to good Jews, Muslims, Buddhists, Hindus or secular people, he humbly replied:

> Those are decisions only the Lord will make. It would be

foolish for me to speculate on who will be there and who
won't … I believe the love of God is absolute. He said he
gave his son for the whole world, and I think he loves
everybody regardless of what label they have.[18]

I agree that God's love is absolute. I also believe God has made his
purpose clear: he sent Christ to save all people, and he promised
victory over every other power in the universe. He guarantees
that one day he will be All in all.

I wouldn't bet against him.

CHAPTER 21

NOW

A life spent making mistakes is not only more honorable,
but more useful than a life spent doing nothing.

— GEORGE BERNARD SHAW

O NLY ONE question remains: *Is Jesus who he claimed to be?*
Each of us must decide for ourselves. But it is important to
recognize that our opinion has absolutely nothing to do with the
answer. Our misunderstandings don't change reality. Our beliefs
have no bearing on whether Jesus will accomplish what he set out
to do. It is either true or false.

Some resist following Christ because they don't like the idea
of change. Relax. Jesus never said we have to sell our car, wear
sandals, or live a perfect life. He simply said to love God and love
our neighbor. This is the only principle we need to be concerned
with: *Love.* The rest is just details. Changes in behavior aren't
a prerequisite for belief in Christ. Our decisions are completely
up to us. We are free to live as we please. God loves each of us
without fail. It is in the comfort of this freedom that we choose
how to live for God, just as a person in love delights in bringing
joy to the object of their affection.[1]

Salvation is guaranteed for all. It is realized the moment we confess Jesus is Lord, and completed upon resurrection. While our choices carry consequences that make life harder or easier, they will never threaten our salvation. It is an irrevocable gift from God, already paid for by the blood of Jesus Christ. Anything we do to honor God can only be an expression of gratitude in response to the love he has already shown.

We are to love our savior, our families, our friends—and our enemies. No one is to be excluded. A life that follows this simple rule is a brilliant source of hope in this age of despair. It will shine. We are to share the good news of God's grace with others who desperately need peace.[2] There is no greater way to thank God for the free gift of salvation than to share his love with others.

When we know the future and understand the full victory of Christ, we are emancipated from the worries of this life. We are unstoppable. We can live a life that reflects the limitless love of God for all mankind, and help others find the truth. And even if we lose our lives doing this, *we win.*

A NEW CREATURE

At the end of this age Christ will return, visible to all, in a way that will leave no doubt as to his identity.[3] No one knows exactly when this will take place.[4] Each person will face the image of the living God, and be judged for the use of our gifts in this life:

> For we must all appear before the judgment seat of Christ, so that each one may receive what is due for what he has done in the body, whether good or evil.[5]

No matter how good, our deeds cannot earn salvation. Only Christ's work on the cross is enough to save us. All we can do is rely on Jesus to provide it. It is never too late to start this new life in Christ, and it only takes a moment to confess that he is Lord of all. One day every knee will bow, and every tongue will confess something that might sound like this:

Dear God, I see that your son Jesus is the Lord and Savior of all, who takes away all mistakes, saves all, and makes all things new. Please pour your spirit into my heart.

Confessing utter reliance on God is really all we can do. We have nothing else to offer. In addition, nothing pleases him more than asking in the name of Jesus Christ, the one he sent to help us. The entire point is to acknowledge the source of all our blessings.

The spirit of the living God immediately fills the heart and dwells inside those who believe and confess that Jesus is Lord.[6] We become a new creature:

> This means that anyone who belongs to Christ has become a new person. The old life is gone; a new life has begun! (2 Corinthians 5:17 NLT)

God's spirit provides peace, abundant life, new strength, and greater understanding today. Although the body remains subject to death and decay in this life, salvation will be completed at the resurrection when we are completely and finally cured.

Maybe you've heard someone mention achievements made with God's help. While some of them may be misunderstood or misattributed, countless astounding things have taken place in the lives of believers: unusual displays of strength, courage, honor, and loyalty. Where our will and ability fall short, the spirit of God can shine. Only in the face of impossible odds can the miraculous occur. Against the all-too-familiar backdrop of failure, the promise of new life is revealed in a believer's prayerful triumphs: beating addiction, healing relationships, finding peace, or simply having hope amid turmoil. We can start to throw the chains off today, and this is only a taste of the full freedom we will eventually enjoy. God is in the business of transformative change, as Saul's life shows. No matter where you are today, remember: *no one* is too far gone. Let God change your story.

The life of the Christian is by no means easier. It can, in fact, be far more difficult. We may stumble, be persecuted, or even lose our lives. But we know the spirit of the creator dwells inside us—the same spirit that brought Jesus back from the grave—and that we, too, will rise again.

> I have told you these things, so that in me you may have peace. In this world you will have trouble. But take heart! I have overcome the world. (John 16:33 NIV)

THE YOUNG BILLIONAIRE

Imagine a child too young to understand that she has been willed a multi-billion-dollar inheritance. Whether this child ever believes or understands this is irrelevant: she is a billionaire. Nothing will change this fact. Her future is sealed.

Similarly, everyone will see the salvation of God.[7] Some will not realize it in this age, whether from stubbornness, laziness, or ignorance. But all people will eventually inherit the gift of everlasting life once they call upon Jesus as Lord and are freed from their bondage to sin and death. We are all billionaires. Most of us just don't realize it yet.

The young billionaire did nothing to earn her wealth. It is a gift. She is merely the beneficiary of work performed by others. Her circumstance now leaves her with a choice: Should she assume a position of superiority over her less fortunate peers? Exude an air of entitlement? Hoard wealth from others because they didn't work hard enough? Or should she, in realizing she has done nothing to deserve her gift, carry herself with humility and help others who are equally undeserving?

The same challenges lie before the heirs of Christ, who have contributed absolutely nothing, yet inherited the largest fortune imaginable. Like the young billionaire, they must also make a choice. Awash in blessing, some Christians have become proud, view themselves as superior, or self-righteously point to their choices and actions. These people are terribly mistaken, and the opportunity to share the good news is lost on them. They fail to see that all people are both equally undeserving and equally important in the eyes of God, and that Jesus Christ values every last one of us as a child created by his own hands.

Possibly the greatest lie advanced by the adversary is that some of us have no value. The world works hard to convince us that those in certain cultures, races, groups, or religions are worthless, yet we are all precious to God. Each and every one of us has value because we were designed in his image. Jesus, the creator, sustainer, and savior of all people, spent his time on earth talking to, walking with, and caring for those he created. He loves all of us without exception. He lived for all people, died for all people, and will not be satisfied until he saves all people.

If only we could see each other as Jesus does, then maybe it would finally be possible for us to cast off our pride, our fear, and our greed—and begin to love like Christ.

YOUR GARDEN

In the opening chapter, we reflected on the relative insignificance the world places upon our lives, and how quickly we are forgotten after death. In reality, your time here is very important. You will face moral challenges, and will be held responsible for the choices you make. Decisions aren't made in a vacuum, and yours will affect the lives of others, both today and for generations to come.

What do you stand for?

Our choices affect more than just a brief life on earth. All will stand before the creator and give an account of our actions. Most of us are myopically focused on our own plight, wasting our lives by wallowing in self-pity, failing to realize how blessed we truly are—or what a blessing we could be to others. Accordingly, when the day of judgment comes, the orphans, the widows, the sick, the maimed, the poor—those we have ignored or stepped over to serve our own self-interests—may be richly rewarded for their unjust suffering, while we who stood by idly receive nothing.

Whom do you serve?

In the Garden of Eden, Adam chose to defy God. Since then, each of us has decided to go our own way—and tasted the bitter misery that results. Today we find ourselves back in that garden, confronted with the same choice: We can either embrace or run from God's love. We missed out on the tree of life in God's first garden, but that's okay. God provided a perfect sacrifice, nailed to a new tree of life. The time has come to call his name.

It's a new beginning. As a new creature, you can choose a better path than Adam did. This is your realm of control, your dominion, your responsibility. With each decision, you lay the foundation for either a lush garden or a winter desert, peace or turmoil, freedom or bondage, order or chaos. You will forge the conditions in which you and those around you must dwell. You are responsible for the reality you are constructing. The stone that the builders rejected seeks to become your cornerstone.[8] Now you must choose whether to take it up or toss it aside.

What is your purpose?

This world and everything in it is out of God, sustained by God, and will be returned to God.[9] All power will be brought under his sovereign authority, but for now, control has temporarily been given to Satan. He offered Jesus all the kingdoms of the world, if only Jesus would bow down and worship him.[10] But Jesus did not settle for anything less than what he was sent to achieve. We shouldn't settle for immediate gratification either. We are to pursue God above, not his creation around us. Nothing this age has to offer can compare to the riches of freedom in Christ.

Jesus fulfilled his purpose—even though the world was aligned against him—and now you must fulfill yours: to love God and love others. This starts with seeing the relentless love God has for every last person, and especially for you. He loved you enough to give his own life for you. He will never stop loving you.

God has won.

NOTES

CHAPTER 1: LIFE

1. "The 2011 Nobel Prize in Physics," Nobel Media AB 2014, October 31, 2011. http://www.nobelprize.org/nobel_prizes/physics/laureates/2011/press.html.
2. "The Final Interview with Stone Phillips," *Dateline NBC* television broadcast, November 29, 1994.
3. "Dahmer Pleads Guilty to 16th," *St. Petersburg Times*, May 2, 1992.
4. Brian Masters, *The Shrine of Jeffrey Dahmer* (London, England: Hodder & Stoughton, 1993), 4.

CHAPTER 2: LOGIC

1. James Randi, *The Faith Healers* (Buffalo, NY: Prometheus Books, 1989).
2. B. Drummond Ayres Jr., "Families Learning of 39 Cultists Who Died Willingly," *New York Times*, March 29, 1997. http://www.nytimes.com/1997/03/29/us/families-learning-of-39-cultists-who-died-willingly.html.
3. A. Rechtschaffen and B. M. Bergmann, "Sleep deprivation in the rat by the disk-over-water method," *Behavioural Brain Research*, July–August 1995, 69(1–2):55–63. PubMed PMID: 7546318.

CHAPTER 3: RELIGIONS

1. "Parents locked son, 13, in basement room for 'disciplinary reasons,' police say," *CNN*, July 10, 2014. http://www.cnn.com/2014/06/26/justice/georgia-boy-locked-in-basement/index.html.
2. John Calvin, vol. 2 of *Institutes of the Christian Religion*, trans. John Allen (Philadelphia, PA: Presbyterian Board of Publication, 1843), 145.
3. Calvin, *Institutes*, 141.
4. Calvin, *Institutes*, 149.
5. Richard Baxter, *The Saints' Everlasting Rest* (London, 1650), 323–4.
6. This quote is often attributed to Blaise Pascal, who actually wrote "Jamais

on ne fait le mal fi pleinement & fi gayement, que quand on le fait par un faux principe de conscience." See Blaise Pascal, *Pensées De Pascal* (Paris: Dezobry et E. Magdeleine, 1852).

7. "Resolution On Racial Reconciliation On The 150th Anniversary Of The Southern Baptist Convention," *Southern Baptist Convention*, 1995. http://www.sbc.net/resolutions/amResolution.asp?ID=899.

8. "CIA World Factbook – Religions," *Central Intelligence Agency*. https://www.cia.gov/library/publications/the-world-factbook/fields/2122.html.

9. If the total number of unique belief systems is represented by the number n, with each one denying the beliefs of the others, then at least $n-1$ of these mutually exclusive explanations must be wrong.

CHAPTER 4: CAUSE

1. "No words to describe monkeys' play," *BBC*, May 9, 2003. http://news.bbc.co.uk/1/hi/3013959.stm.

2. Steven H. Strogatz, *Sync: The Emerging Science of Spontaneous Order* (New York: Hyperion, 2003), 1.

3. "The 2011 Nobel Prize in Physics – Press Release," Nobel Media AB 2014, Oct 31, 2011. http://www.nobelprize.org/nobel_prizes/physics/laureates/2011/press.html.

4. Xuan Thuan Trinh, *Science & the Search for Meaning: Perspectives from International Scientists* (Philadelphia: Templeton Foundation Press, 2006), 186.

5. Stephen Hawking and Leonard Mlodinow, *The Grand Design* (New York: Random House Pub., 2010), 180.

6. Nick Watt, "Stephen Hawking: 'Science Makes God Unnecessary'," *ABC News*, September 7, 2010. http://abcnews.go.com/GMA/stephen-hawking-science-makes-god-unnecessary/story?id=11571150.

7. Rebecca J. Rosen, "Einstein Likely Never Said One of His Most Oft-Quoted Phrases," *The Atlantic*, Aug 9, 2013. http://www.theatlantic.com/technology/archive/2013/08/einstein-likely-never-said-one-of-his-most-oft-quoted-phrases/278508/.

8. "Goal 1: Understand the nature and distribution of habitable environments in the Universe," *Astrobiology: Roadmap*, NASA, http://astrobiology.arc.nasa.gov/roadmap/g1.html.

9. Some have argued that these requirements may not be necessary for other life forms. This assertion *increases* the odds of finding life in the cosmos, which compounds the problem since we have found none.

10. Leroy Hood and David Galas, "The Digital Code of DNA," *Nature* 421.6921 (2003), 440–4.

11. Machine learning and artificial intelligence require some sort of initial hard-

ware and an algorithm to operate, even if they are able to output valid code. A system doesn't simply bootstrap itself into functionality.

12. "Background on Comparative Genomic Analysis," *National Human Genome Research Institute*, December 2002. http://www.genome.gov/10005835.

13. C. B. Ruff, E. Trinkaus, and T. W. Holliday, "Body Mass and Encephalization in Pleistocene Homo," *Nature*, 387 (May 8, 1997), 173–176; J. Kappleman, "They Might be Giants," *Nature*, 387 (May 8, 1997), 126–127; A. Gibbon, "Bone Sizes Trace the Decline of Man (and Woman)," *Science*, 276 (May 9, 1997), 896–897.

14. Joel Achenbach, "Worlds Away," *Washington Post*, April 23, 2006, W15.

15. "More Than 9 in 10 Americans Continue to Believe in God," Gallup, Inc., June 3, 2011. http://www.gallup.com/poll/147887/americans-continue-believe-god.aspx.

CHAPTER 5: MESSAGE

1. M. West, *Studies in the Text and Transmission of the Iliad* (München: K.G. Saur, 2001), 87. West catalogs other finds including an additional 840 unpublished papyri fragments found in Oxyrhynchus, Egypt, which are presently being held at the Ashmolean Museum in Oxford, England.

2. Most religions are in agreement as to which works should be included, although some extra books appear in the Catholic Bible. These additional works are often referred to as the *apocrypha*.

3. Jon Krakauer, *Under the Banner of Heaven: A Story of Violent Faith* (New York: Anchor Books, 2004), 5–6.

4. Abby Ohlheiser, "The Mormon church finally acknowledges founder Joseph Smith's polygamy," *Washington Post*, Nov 11, 2014. http://www.washington post.com/news/national/wp/2014/11/11/the-mormon-church-finally-ackno wledges-founder-joseph-smiths-polygamy/.

5. Jews do not, however, believe the second half of the modern Bible (the New Testament) to be inspired by God. And while Muslims view the entire Bible as divinely inspired, they generally believe it has been corrupted by men, and the Koran provides new guidance.

6. Mark 10:6

7. Isaiah 40:22

CHAPTER 6: CONTACT

1. If AD meant "after death," there would be no way to indicate years AD 1–33, which was the period spanning Jesus' life. There is no year zero; the calendar advances from 1 BC to AD 1. Most historians agree that Jesus was born about 1–3 BC.

2. The Book of Isaiah foretells many signs of the expected messiah, which Jews see as yet unfulfilled. They continue to anticipate their leader. Christians, however, maintain that Jesus is the Christ, and will return in the future to rule over the earth.

3. In the interest of brevity we do not cover them all here. See, e.g., John 5:17–18,23–24; 8:19; 14:1–9; 19:7; 20:27–29; and Matthew 27:43. Even in the absence of this extensive record, there can be no question that Jesus claimed to be God, since this was precisely the basis for his trial and execution.

4. C. S. Lewis, Mere Christianity (New York, NY: HarperOne, 2015), 52.

5. Flavius Josephus, *The Works of Flavius Josephus; Comprising the Antiquities of the Jews*, trans. William Whiston (London: Willoughby & Company, 1840), 425.

6. Josephus, *Antiquities of the Jews*, 381.

7. A frequently cited passage begins "Now, there was about this time Jesus..." (Josephus, 377–378). Its authenticity has been called into question, as some text may have been added to subsequent manuscripts to speak favorably of Jesus. The fact that textual critics can determine such things underscores the reliability of the other passages cited here, which have also been thoroughly analyzed. There is no need to rely on a disputed passage; there are many more to choose from.

8. Cornelius Tacitus, *Annals of Tacitus*, trans. Alfred John Church and William Jackson Brodribb (London: Macmillan and Company, 1921), 304–305.

9. A handful of people have questioned the spelling used in a manuscript that may read "Chrestians" rather than "Christians," and have suggested this is not a reference to Jesus and his followers. It is quite telling that this is the only argument one is left with after reading this passage.

10. Temple Chevallier, *A Translation of the Epistles of Clement of Rome, Polycarp, and Ignatius* (Cambridge: J. & J. J. Deighton, 1833), 500–501.

11. Chevallier, 501–502.

12. Lucian of Samosata, *The Works of Lucian of Samosata, Vol. 4*, trans. H. W. Fowler and F. G. Fowler, 4 vols. (Oxford: Clarendon Press, 1905), 82–83.

13. References to these events appear in *Chronografiai* 18.1.

14. John 19:6–10 NIV

15. John 19:19–22

16. Mark 15:30

CHAPTER 7: MYSTERY

1. John 12:34 NIV

2. Luke 22:61

3. Judas Iscariot, the disciple who had betrayed Jesus, was no longer counted among the twelve disciples, and took his own life soon after.
4. 1 Corinthians 15:14 NIV
5. Chevallier, *Epistles*, 100.
6. We can expect most writings that corroborate belief in Jesus' resurrection to be written by Christians. It is unlikely for someone who has no interest in the matter—or is vehemently opposed to it—to be a credible source of information on the beliefs and practices of the Christian community.
7. 1 Corinthians 15:4–7 NIV
8. John 20:13–16
9. Mark 15:39
10. John 19:33–34
11. Matthew 27:62–66
12. Matthew 28:11–15
13. John 20:24–29
14. Acts 6:7
15. John 5:46–47 NIV
16. Psalm 22:6–8,14–18 NLT
17. Isaiah 7:14. See Matthew 1:16–25.
18. Micah 5:2. See Matthew 2:1.
19. Genesis 22:15–18; Numbers 24:17; Jeremiah 23:5. See Matthew 1:1; Luke 3:23–34.
20. Psalm 2:7. See Matthew 3:17.
21. Micah 5:2. See Colossians 1:17; John 1:1.
22. Psalm 110:1; Isaiah 7:14. See Luke 20:41–44; Matthew 1:23.
23. Deuteronomy 18:18. See Matthew 21:11.
24. Isaiah 33:22. See Matthew 27:37.
25. Isaiah 9:1–2. See Matthew 4:12–17.
26. Isaiah 35:5–6. See Matthew 9:35.
27. Zechariah 9:9. See Luke 19:35–37.
28. Psalm 118:22. See 1 Peter 2:7–8.
29. Psalm 16:10. See Acts 2:31.
30. Josh McDowell, *The New Evidence That Demands a Verdict* (Nashville, TN: T. Nelson, 1999), 183–192.
31. Psalm 41:9. See Matthew 10:2–4.
32. Zechariah 11:12. See Matthew 26:15.
33. Zechariah 11:13. See Matthew 27:5.
34. Zechariah 11:13. See Matthew 27:6–8.
35. Zechariah 13:7. See Mark 14:50.
36. Psalm 35:11. See Matthew 26:59–61.

37. Isaiah 53:7. See Matthew 27:12–19.
38. Isaiah 53:5. See Matthew 27:26.
39. Isaiah 50:6; Micah 5:1. See Matthew 26:67.
40. Psalm 22:7–8. See Matthew 27:31.
41. Psalm 109:24. See John 19:17; Luke 23:26.
42. Psalm 22:16. See Luke 23:33; John 20:25.
43. Isaiah 53:12. See Matthew 27:38.
44. Isaiah 53:12. See Luke 23:34.
45. Isaiah 53:3. See John 7:5,48.
46. Psalm 69:4. See John 15:25.
47. Psalm 38:11. See Luke 23:49.
48. Psalm 109:25. See Matthew 27:39.
49. Psalm 22:17. See Luke 23:35.
50. Psalm 22:18. See John 19:23–24.
51. Psalm 69:21. See John 19:28.
52. Psalm 69:21. See Matthew 27:34.
53. Psalm 22:1. See Matthew 27:46.
54. Psalm 31:5. See Luke 23:46.
55. Psalm 34:20. See John 19:33.
56. Psalm 22:14. See John 19:34.
57. Zechariah 12:10. See John 19:34.
58. Amos 8:9. See Matthew 27:45.
59. Isaiah 53:9. See Matthew 27:57–60.
60. See, e.g., Lee Strobel, *The Case for Christ: A Journalist's Personal Investigation of the Evidence for Jesus* (Grand Rapids, MI: Zondervan, 1998). While Strobel's works are illuminating, it should be noted that I have spoken with him on the topic of this book, and like most modern evangelicals, he rejects the assertion that Christ will ultimately defeat sin and death.

CHAPTER 8: DEITY

1. Genesis 1:2. Strong's Concordance also offers *breath, mind,* and *spirit* as translations for H7307 (*ruwach*)—all intangible and invisible, like the wind.
2. 2 Corinthians 4:4
3. John 1:14; Matthew 27:40
4. See John 1:1–2, which describes the Word of God (*Logos*, or λόγος) coexisting with God before creation. Accordingly, it is believed that the pre-incarnate Jesus is who walked with Adam and Eve in the Garden of Eden and appeared before Abram, prior to ever being born in the flesh.
5. John 8:57–58
6. John 1:3; Colossians 1:16–17

7. See, e.g., Matthew 28:19; 1 Corinthians 6:11; 12:3.
8. 1 Thessalonians 5:23
9. We must tread carefully here. For example, a phrase in 1 John 5:7 that was very influential in developing the Trinitarian view is missing from most manuscripts.
10. It is difficult to convey the nature of an eternal, omnipresent, omnipotent deity in any language. As God simply says, "I AM THAT I AM."
11. Deuteronomy 4:2; Revelation 22:18–19
12. John 3:16
13. John 14:6
14. Psalm 90:2; Revelation 1:4
15. Isaiah 46:9–10; Hebrews 4:13; 1 John 3:20
16. Psalm 139:7–12
17. Ephesians 1:11; Luke 1:37
18. 1 John 4:7–8; Psalm 136:26; John 3:16
19. Psalm 40:5; 145:17; Deuteronomy 32:4
20. Job 34:10; Psalm 5:4
21. Malachi 3:6; James 1:17; Hebrews 13:8
22. John 1:3
23. Hebrews 2:10
24. Alternatively, one could assert God is fully capable of doing anything he pleases, but thankfully chooses never to do certain things. Whether his choices establish his nature or his nature establishes his choices is moot—he is perfect.

CHAPTER 9: EVIL

1. 1 John 1:5
2. See Strong's H7451.
3. John 12:31; 14:30; 16:11; 2 Corinthians 4:4
4. Matthew 4:8–11
5. These verses may allude to an antichrist figure rather than Satan.
6. See Isaiah 14:12. The original word *heylel* (Strong's H1966) merely means a bright shining one or a light-bearer, just as Christ is described in Revelation 22:16. *Lucifer* as a name for Satan is deeply rooted in mythology rather than the original text of the Bible.
7. 2 Corinthians 11:14
8. See Strong's H1281 (*bariyach*) and H2490 (*chalal*). Some versions render this as "pierced the fleeing serpent." Whether formed, profaned, began, or pierced, it is clear that God alone holds power over this creature.
9. Genesis 2:7

10. Revelation 12:3–4. Whether the result of the adversary's deception or willful rebellion, these creatures—like Adam—likely had a choice.
11. Luke 22:31; Job 2:1–7
12. Luke 22:31–32
13. See Job chapter 1. Some wish to distinguish that Job had a hedge of protection. Regardless, God took an action that permitted Satan to do damage that could not otherwise have resulted.

CHAPTER 10: IMPERFECTION

1. Genesis 1:31
2. Genesis 3:1–7 ESV
3. Genesis 2:17
4. Genesis 50:20; Psalm 119:71
5. Genesis 3:22–24
6. For an in-depth look at how sin and evil relate to God's plan, see A. E. Knoch, *The Problem of Evil and the Judgments of God* (Santa Clarita, CA: Concordant Publishing Concern, 2008).
7. Judges 20:16
8. James 1:13
9. Romans 3:23
10. Romans 6:23; James 1:14–15
11. Except for Jesus Christ, who was not born of an earthly father.
12. See Genesis 3:16–17; 1 Corinthians 11:3–9; and Colossians 3:18.
13. Psalm 51:5
14. Romans 7:18–19 ESV
15. Isaiah 59:1–2; Romans 3:23

CHAPTER 11: POWER

1. Job 23:13; 42:2
2. Genesis 3:7
3. Hebrews 9:22
4. See Isaiah 53:10. Isaiah 53 contains a fascinating summary of God's future deliverance of mankind from corruption, written hundreds of years before Jesus' birth and crucifixion.
5. John 1:29
6. 2 Corinthians 5:21
7. See John 19:30. The Greek reads Τετέλεσται (*tetelestai*), which may also be interpreted as "paid in full."
8. Hebrews 7:26–27

9. This is similar to how God used Joseph to save many lives, even though his brothers sought to do him harm. See Genesis 50:20.

10. Revelation 13:8

CHAPTER 12: OPTIONS

1. The interested reader can look to resources on *limited atonement.*

2. 2 Peter 3:9

3. 1 Timothy 2:1–6

4. According to this view, man's free will would be violated if God were to save him against his will; God is therefore powerless to save a man who chooses to reject Jesus' sacrifice. Alternatively, one could assert that God certainly has the power, but lacks the desire to overcome man's free will—a position that suffers the same fate as the first option.

5. Job 42:2

CHAPTER 13: VICTORY

1. John 14:6 NIV

2. 1 John 4:15

3. 1 John 4:14

4. John 12:32 NIV. The word "draw" comes from the Greek *helkuo*, which can also be translated "drag"—a graphic description of Jesus' determination.

5. John 17:20–23; 10:16

6. Ephesians 1:11

7. 1 Samuel 13:14; Acts 13:22

8. See, e.g., Romans 10:9–10; and 1 John 4:15.

9. John 8:32

10. 1 Corinthians 12:3

11. Romans 8:9

12. John 3:17

13. John 6:37

14. Hebrews 13:8

15. Philippians 2:9–11; Revelation 5:13

16. 1 Peter 3:18 contains ζῳοποιηθείς, the root of which is Strong's G2227.

17. Acts 1:9–11; Romans 8:34

18. Romans 6:23

19. Thomas Allin, *Christ Triumphant* (Canyon Country, CA: Concordant Publishing Concern, 1994), Reprint of the 9th edition, vii.

CHAPTER 14: HISTORY

1. Clement of Alexandria, *Stromata VII*, Chapter 2.

2. Clement of Alexandria, *Fragments III*, Comments on the First Epistle of John Chap. ii. Ver. 2.
3. Origen, *De Principiis I*, Chapter VI: On the End or Consummation.
4. Origen, *Contra Celsus VIII*, Chapter LXXII.
5. Hosea Ballou, *The Ancient History of Universalism* (Boston: Marsh and Capen, 1829), 114–115.
6. Ballou, 169.
7. Gregory of Nyssa, *Tract. In dictum Apostoli,* Tunc etiam ipse Filius subjicietur Patri.
8. Gregory of Nyssa, *Oratio Catechetica*, Chapter 26.
9. While early Christian teachers held that all people would eventually be saved and received into bliss, this outcome was believed to follow a period of corrective discipline. Opinions on the sufferings of the wicked varied from cleansing in a mild purgatory to a long and excruciating trial by fire in a future age. Ultimately, though, they would succeed in healing the afflicted—and then cease.
10. Basil the Great, *De Ascetics*.
11. Saint Jerome, *Homily on Jonah*.
12. Augustine, *Enchirdion CXII*.
13. John Wesley Hanson, *Universalism: The Prevailing Doctrine Of The Christian Church During Its First Five Hundred Years* (Boston and Chicago: Universalist Publishing House, 1899), 53.
14. Hosea Ballou, *The Ancient History of Universalism* (Boston: Marsh and Capen, 1829).
15. Thomas Allin, *Christ Triumphant* (Canyon Country, CA: Concordant Publishing Concern, 1994), Reprint of the 9th edition.
16. Thomas Baldwin Thayer, *The Origin and History of the Doctrine of Endless Punishment* (Boston: Universalist Publishing House, 1855).
17. Edward Beecher, *History of Opinions on the Scriptural Doctrine of Retribution* (New York: Appleton, 1878), 189.
18. 1 Timothy 2:1–6

CHAPTER 15: LOVE

1. 1 Corinthians 13:4–8 NIV
2. Matthew 22:37–40
3. 1 Corinthians 13:13
4. Ezekiel 18:4
5. Ecclesiastes 12:7
6. Genesis 1:27
7. Romans 14:7–9

8. 1 Timothy 5:8
9. Luke 23:34
10. John 3:17
11. 1 Chronicles 16:34,41
12. Revelation 21:5 NIV

CHAPTER 16: GRACE

1. "Azim Khamisa & Ples Felix (USA)," *The Forgiveness Project*, March 29, 1997. http://theforgivenessproject.com/stories/azim-khamisa-ples-felix-usa/.
2. Exodus 21:24; Leviticus 24:20; Deuteronomy 19:21
3. Romans 5:18 NIV
4. The word δικαίωσιν, derived from *dikaiōsis* (Strong's G1347), could also be rendered "acquittal." Romans 4:25 uses the same word to guarantee justification for believers.
5. 1 Corinthians 15:45
6. 1 Corinthians 15:21
7. The first Adam passed iniquity to mankind, which continues to be transmitted through each male descendant. The Son of God was born unto a virgin woman and had no earthly father. Only Adam and Christ were not born in sin—no one else had a choice.
8. Colossians 1:15–17 ESV
9. 1 Corinthians 15:42–44
10. Romans 8:19–21
11. James 2:19; Mark 3:11. We are not told why these members of creation chose to align themselves with the adversary. It is possible that they were deceived—much like Adam and Eve—and remain in a state of defection despite realizing the truth. Regardless, if they have knees or tongues, we are promised that they will ultimately confess Jesus Christ is Lord, resulting in salvation (Romans 10:9).
12. Revelation 12:12
13. John 10:27–30
14. Romans 8:28–30
15. 1 Corinthians 13:8–13
16. Hebrews 9:27. Believers alive at Christ's return are the only exception. Further, the unsaved will die a second death (Revelation 2:11; 20:6,14; 21:8).
17. 1 John 3:2; Philippians 3:20–21
18. Romans 3:24; 5:15–18; Ephesians 2:8–9
19. Many translations indicate that Jesus said "it is hard for you to kick against the pricks." This metaphorically describes the fruitless fight of an ox against its master—or the futility of resisting God.

20. An unbeliever cannot understand spiritual things (1 Corinthians 2:14), does not seek God (Romans 3:10–12), and is a slave of sin (Romans 6:14–20).
21. Hebrews 12:2; Romans 12:3
22. Ephesians 2:8–9
23. John 6:44,65; Matthew 11:27
24. Matthew 22:14 reads, "For many are called, but few are chosen." Clearly God is the one doing the calling and the choosing here, rather than man.
25. Some assert that works are necessary to gain salvation since James 2:14–26 states that faith without works is dead. While true faith bears the fruit of good works, and obedience can deepen one's faith, our works contribute nothing to Christ's sacrifice on the cross.
26. Romans 11:29
27. 1 Corinthians 15:22–26
28. Genesis 19:24–25
29. Ezekiel 16:53–55
30. Matthew 11:23

CHAPTER 17: FREEDOM

1. Romans 10:13
2. "The Final Interview with Stone Phillips," *Dateline NBC* television broadcast, November 29, 1994.
3. Romans 4:4–5
4. Matthew 7:1–5
5. Romans 3:23
6. Jeremiah 10:23
7. Proverbs 16:9; 21:1
8. 1 Samuel 2:6
9. 2 Samuel 14:14
10. Hebrews 13:8
11. Romans 8:11
12. Early Church Faith. "Brad Jersak - The Gospel in Chairs - Session 1 (FGC 2016)." YouTube Video, 29:47. June 29, 2017. https://www.youtube.com/watch?v=N7FKhHScgUQ.

CHAPTER 18: TIME

1. See Strong's G2889 and G165, respectively.
2. The author's meticulous efforts are similarly thwarted by translators throughout the King James Version. See, e.g., Revelation 11:15, Titus 1:2, and John 3:15–16.
3. A closer match for "eternal" may be the Greek word ἀΐδιος (Strong's G126),

in which case *eternal* should appear just twice in the King James Version's New Testament—only in Romans 1:20 and Jude 1:6—rather than forty-five times in reference to many things that are undeniably temporal. Note that referring to the creator as the "God of the ages" is distinctly different from invoking *eternity*, though equally accurate: doing so does not deny that God is eternal; it merely emphasizes that God created the ages, just as he is God of mankind or God of all creation.

4. Jonah 2:6
5. Exodus 21:6
6. 1 Kings 8:13, 9:3
7. Exodus 40:15; Hebrews 7:11–18
8. In these instances, the original Hebrew words are based on *'owlam* (עוֹלָם), Strong's H5769. In any case, it is abundantly clear from the context that "forever" is not the intended meaning.
9. The original Greek phrase is εἰς τοὺς αἰῶνας τῶν αἰώνων.
10. John Wesley Hanson, *Aiōn-Aiōnios: An Excursus on the Greek Word Rendered Everlasting, Eternal, Etc., in the Holy Bible* (Chicago: Jansen, McClurg, & Company, 1880).
11. Edward Beecher, *History of Opinions on the Scriptural Doctrine of Retribution* (New York: D. Appleton and Company, 1878).
12. Charles H. Pridgeon, *Is Hell Eternal: Or, Will God's Plan Fail?* (New York and London: Funk & Wagnalls, 1920).
13. G. Campbell Morgan, *God's Methods With Man in Time: Past, Present, and Future* (E. Northfield, Mass: Fleming H. Revell Company, 1898), 185–186.
14. Hebrews 1:2. It is critical to study with an accurate translation. Some use "world" instead of "ages," which loses the point completely.
15. 1 Corinthians 2:7. Note that what is being discussed as existing before time began is the only thing that could exist outside of time: God. See also 2 Timothy 1:9 and Titus 1:2.
16. Matthew 12:32; Mark 10:30; Luke 18:30
17. Hebrews 9:26. It is difficult for us to fully comprehend what this means, but this verse appears to describe the end of any necessity for time.
18. Ephesians 1:10–11
19. Ephesians 3:8–11. Consistent, accurate translations will use "ages" rather than "world" and "eternal."
20. Hebrews 10:1–18
21. Romans 14:1–23; Mark 7:15–20

CHAPTER 19: JUSTICE

1. Colossians 1:20

2. Acts 24:15

3. John 5:28–29

4. Revelation 20:4–5. God ascribed righteousness to those (such as Abraham, Moses, and David) who placed their faith in God's promise to deliver a messiah, even though the name of Jesus wasn't known to them. God's provision for those who relied entirely on his promise of deliverance transcended the chronology of these events. It is their faith in God alone that saved them. Now that the Christ has been revealed, our faith is placed in Jesus.

5. 1 Corinthians 15:35–49

6. John 5:24; 1 Corinthians 15:50–55

7. Revelation 20:6

8. Revelation 20:5

9. Romans 6:3–10; 2 Samuel 14:14

10. Revelation 21:8

11. Matthew 8:12; 10:28; 13:40–43; 18:8; 22:13; Jude 1:7; Hebrews 9:27; 10:31; 2 Peter 2:4; Revelation 19:20; 20:15; 21:8.

12. Mark 9:49

13. Revelation 2:11

14. Isaiah 48:10; Malachai 3:2–3; 1 Peter 1:7; Jeremiah 9:6–7

15. Isaiah 1:25 NIV

16. Deuteronomy 7:6–8

17. Hebrews 12:29. God is eternal and is described as a consuming fire, so any references to "everlasting" or "eternal" fire make sense. However, it does not logically follow that everything exposed to it will be left in the fire to burn forever.

18. Exodus 15:26; Mark 2:17; Hosea 6:1

19. Revelation 20:13–15

20. The King James Version translates Strong's H7585 (*sheol*) as grave (×31), hell (×31), and pit (×3); and Strong's G86 (*hades*) as hell (×10) and grave (×1).

21. Acts 13:22 ESV

22. "And ye, in putting them [the departed souls] in heaven, hell, and purgatory, destroy the arguments wherewith Christ and Paul prove the resurrection. … And then what cause is there of the resurrection?" (William Tyndale, *An Answer to Sir Thomas More's Dialogue*, Parker's 1850 reprint, bk. 4, ch. 4, pp. 180,181.)

23. See Martin Luther, *An Exposition of Salomon's Booke, called Ecclesiastes or the Preacher*, 1553, folio 151v. The 1573 English translation is modernized here for the reader's sake. A number of Luther's writings describe soul sleep.

24. See Strong's H8064 (*shamayim*) and Strong's G3772 (*ouranos*), both of which

represent the sky and all things visible in it—not paradise—582 times in the King James Version.

25. Revelation 21:1–3
26. 2 Corinthians 5:10; Romans 14:10–12
27. Matthew 25:14–30
28. Revelation 4:10
29. Job 5:17–18
30. Zephaniah 3:7–9
31. Isaiah 54:7–8
32. See Strong's G1067 (*geenna*), Strong's H7585 (*shĕ'owl*), and Strong's G86 (*hadēs*). Strong's G5020 (*tartaroō*) is also the name of a specific location. There is no need to delve too deeply their meanings, since it is sufficient for the present inquiry to demonstrate limited duration for all judgments. Whatever they are, they will one day come to an end.
33. The original Greek is αἰῶνας αἰώνων.
34. "For ever and ever" also makes little sense; it is redundant and imprecise, where "forever" would have sufficed—if in fact that were what *aiōn* really meant.
35. See Strong's G4383. Also the word translated "from" is based on Strong's G575 (ἀπό), and refers to the origin from which something comes.
36. See Strong's G2851 (κόλασις) and G2849 (κολάζω). Cf. G5098 (τιμωρία) and G5097 (τιμωρέω).
37. Ephesians 2:8–9
38. Matthew 13:34 NIV
39. See Strong's G2976.
40. This concept is incompatible with the modern creed, which teaches that the saved will not grieve for the lost because they will not remember them—one of many inconsistencies presented by today's Christian lore.
41. This view, termed "the doctrine of the immortality of the soul," has no need for Christ's resurrection, since life is already endless. Cf. Psalm 6:5; 115:17; 146:3–4; Ecclesiastes 12:1–7; Job 14:21; John 11:11–14.
42. For a thorough list see D. P. Livermore, *Proof Texts of Endless Punishment, Examined and Explained* (Chicago, IL: S. & A. Emerson Printers, 1862).
43. C. S. Lewis, *The Problem of Pain* (New York, NY: HarperOne, 2001), 130.
44. Proverbs 9:10
45. 1 John 4:18; Romans 8:15
46. Matthew 22:36–40
47. Psalm 30:5
48. Matthew 5:26; Luke 12:59
49. James 3:17; Ezekiel 33:11

CHAPTER 20: DARKNESS

1. John 3:19
2. Charles H. Spurgeon, *The Soul-Winner* (New York, NY: Fleming H. Revell Company, 1895), 167.
3. Livermore, iii–iv.
4. Colossians 2:8
5. Mark 7:6–13
6. 1 Timothy 4:1–12
7. Matthew 20:15–16 ESV
8. 2 Corinthians 5:18–20
9. 1 Corinthians 13:12
10. 1 John 4:19
11. Romans 10:9–13; 1 John 4:15
12. 1 Corinthians 15:25
13. Revelation 5:12–13
14. "Evangelism Is Most Effective Among Kids," The Barna Group, Ltd., October 11, 2004. https://www.barna.com/research/evangelism-is-most-effective-among-kids/.
15. Matthew 18:3,6; 19:14; 21:16; Mark 10:13–16; Luke 18:17
16. Charles Darwin, Nora Barlow (ed.), *The Autobiography of Charles Darwin 1809–1882: With Original Omissions Restored* (London: Collins, 1958), 87.
17. Isaiah 55:8–11. In a breathtaking example of our blindness, this verse has been cited by Christians in *defense* of everlasting torment.
18. "Pilgrim's Progress," *Newsweek*, August 13, 2006. https://www.newsweek.com/pilgrims-progress-109171.

CHAPTER 21: NOW

1. See Ephesians chapter 4.
2. 2 Corinthians 5:19–21
3. Revelation 1:7; Matthew 16:27, 24:27, 24:30–31
4. Matthew 24:44
5. 2 Corinthians 5:10 ESV
6. 1 Corinthians 3:16; Ephesians 1:13; John 14:26–27
7. Luke 3:5–6
8. Acts 8:11
9. Romans 11:36
10. Matthew 4:8–11

Find out more at

believablebook.com